Advance Praise for
The Death of You

"Miguel handles the subject of death in a mature, positive way and gives the reader tools to assist with their own worries on the matter. If Miguel would write about taxes I could have all of my bases covered."

—Donivan Blair, bassist for the Toadies and author of *Even If It Kills Me: Martial Arts, Rock and Roll, and Mortality*

"Miguel Chen has gifted us a courageous, unflinching, and oddly comforting practical guide to death—how to accept it, how to live with it, and how to grow from it. This book may very well change how you look at death."

—Jonathan Evison, author of *The Revised Fundamentals of Caregiving*

"*The Death of You* proves to be the perfect foil to the idea of living fast and dying young. Miguel provides a nice roadmap for the inevitable maturity and mortality we all find ourselves facing."

—Kyle Kinane, comedian

The Death of You

A Book for Anyone Who Might Not Live Forever

MIGUEL CHEN

with

ROD MEADE SPERRY

Wisdom

Wisdom Publications
199 Elm Street
Somerville, MA 02144 USA
wisdompubs.org

Library of Congress Cataloging-in-Publication Data
Names: Chen, Miguel, author. | Meade Sperry, Rod, author.
Title: The death of you: a book for anyone who might not live forever /
Miguel Chen with Rod Meade Sperry.
Description: Somerville, MA: Wisdom Publications, [2019] |
Includes bibliographical references. |
Identifiers: LCCN 2019000214 (print) | LCCN 2019010905 (ebook) |
ISBN 9781614295983 (ebook) | ISBN 9781614295747 (pbk.: alk. paper)
Subjects: LCSH: Death—Religious aspects—Buddhism. |
Death—Meditations.
Classification: LCC BQ4487 (ebook) | LCC BQ4487 .C47 2019 (print) |
DDC 294.3/423—dc23
LC record available at https://lccn.loc.gov/2019000214

ISBN 978-1-61429-574-7   ebook ISBN 978-1-61429-598-3

23 22 21 20 19   5 4 3 2 1

Cover design by Marc Whitaker. Interior design by James D. Skatges.
Set in Minion 3 8/10.

MIX
Paper from
responsible sources
FSC
www.fsc.org   FSC® C005010

Please visit fscus.org.

For my mother Esther, sister Ana,
best friend Brandon, and all of the many,
many loved ones we've lost along the way.

There is no such thing as inner peace.
There is only nervousness or death.
Any attempt to prove otherwise
constitutes unacceptable behavior.
—FRAN LEBOWITZ

Death is perfectly safe.
—STEPHEN LEVINE

Contents

1

You Wake Up

Dimly for thirty years;
Faintly for thirty years—
Dimly and faintly for sixty years:
At my death I pass my feces and offer them
    to Brahma.

—IKKYU (1394–1481),
written as his own death approached

YOU WAKE UP and get ready for your day: bathroom, shower, breakfast, brush teeth, walk the dogs, and go. You're off to work.

You spend your day at a job which, let's say, you don't hate. Maybe you even like it, a little or a lot.

You get off work and go home to your family, or your partner, or your dogs, or your plants. You have dinner, spend some time unwinding, go to bed.

You wake up. Repeat.

Repeat, repeat, repeat, repeat.

Then, one day, you don't wake up.

Because you're dead.

You *don't* get up to use the bathroom, or shower, or have breakfast, or walk the dog.

You *don't* go to work, and it doesn't matter if you liked your job—not anymore. You don't go home to your family, or your partner, or your dogs, or your plants. You don't have dinner, or unwind, or go to bed. None of those human concerns are yours anymore.

It doesn't really matter how you died. Maybe you had a heart attack in your sleep. Maybe a deranged lunatic suffocated you with your own pillow. Maybe you unleashed Death-Fart 5000 in a dream and it actually killed you. The deed is done. Your life is over and nothing will change that.

So . . . what now?

Well, your family and friends are, probably, supremely sad. You'd like to tell them it's okay, but you know, you're dead. Plus: *Is* it okay?

The dogs will to have to find someone else to walk them, because you won't be walking anytime soon. Or, ever.

Work might be wondering why you didn't show up. So what if they are? What are they gonna do? Fire you? There's no more work, no more play. Unless you think the act of physically decaying is play.

Your body will start to deteriorate, your flesh rotting away from the bone. You'll surely let out a few last ghastly farts as the wind clears from your system. Finally, after your hair and nails go, there'll be just a horizontal scaffolding of bones. Besides that, in a sense, all that remain are the memories held by those who you affected.

Some of those memories might be really pleasant. Some might be downright awful. Doesn't make much of a difference now, because (*have I mentioned?*) you're dead. How people want to remember you is up to them, and there's nothing you can do to change it now. They get to wake up and live with, or deny, your memory and your impact. You pretty much just get to be dead.

There was still so much you wanted to do! So many places you never got to see! Your children (or your dogs or your plants) will have to grow up without you. Your partner, your loved ones will have to work through their pain and find a way forward. All your plans . . . *poof.*

It's a shame, too: you tried your best in life. You honestly did. You wanted to be a good friend, maybe a good parent, tried at least a little to be an inspiration to others. You worked hard every day to make the most of your time and leave your mark on this earth. Maybe you succeeded, but how could you know that now? To someone who's not alive, could it even matter?

"What now?" = "Where next?"

When you're talking about death, "What now?" can also mean, "Where next?" Does the end of your life mark the beginning of something else? Maybe an eternity of bliss? Will you be reunited with all your deceased loved ones? Is there some white light waiting to take you to heaven, where you'll spend eternity floating on a cloud and eating from an endless taco buffet?

Or maybe you're off to hell. Have you considered the possibility that you've pretty much been an asshole and you're going to burn for it? It's worth considering! You might be headed to an eternity of excruciating pain and suffering, payback for all your sins. Bummer.

Maybe you'll end up in line, waiting to be reborn as a puppy, a snake, a dust mite, or another human. If rebirth or reincarnation is next, will you remember this most recent life? Will your mind, and your slate, be wiped clean?

What if what's next is *nothing*? Maybe you don't even *know* you're dead, because when your body died everything about you ceased to exist. You're rotting in some grave with no idea what's going on. Almost seems like a relief!

But then, what if the exact opposite has happened, and rather than being reduced to nothing, you've expanded into *universe itself*, the only thing that's actually died is the illusion of an individual "self"—and now you've finally come home to your true, ultimate nature. Maybe consciousness belongs to the universe itself and can see in all directions, understand everything—and your life was ultimately a sort of game you played with yourself. That sounds pretty good too.

Or something else entirely?

So what's it gonna be?

There is, of course, not a single person on this planet who can tell us for sure what will happen when we die—though people do have views, some of them quite strong. By the time anyone finds out for sure, it's, well, a little too late to do much with the information. And so the rest of us are left to wonder and, if we're feeling brave, to explore.

Helping you be brave and explore is what this book aims to do. Together, you and I are going to look at all our ideas about death, so that you can make your own decisions about what its meaning is for you and how to your live life right now knowing that, no two ways about it, death is waiting for you at the end. Our friends will die, our perceived enemies will die, our dogs will die, our loved ones and family will die, *WE* will die.

Jeez, Miguel, you say. *This is a huge bummer.*

I hear ya—but it doesn't have to be. Really. Yes, death breaks our hearts, but it doesn't have to destroy us. I've had some serious experience with death, and I'd go so far as to say that connecting with it is what's really brought me to life. There is so much freedom that arises from facing our fears, and if our biggest fear is death, then it seems crazy not to get comfortable with it.

We can even learn to laugh about it.

Now, dust off your farty old corpse, and let's do this.

2

Why Me?

I'm gonna make my death fun. Because we're all gonna die; why not have fun with it?

Why do we worry all the way up until the death? We worry, worry, worry, then we die and we're like: See? I told you I'd die!

—KYLE CEASE

I'M WRITING THIS book because I see a big problem. Death is all around us and we all seem to refuse to look it in the eye. Like we imagine that if we avoid thinking about death, we somehow won't ever have to deal with it. But you and I both know that's wrong.

I'm not saying we need to become death-obsessed, constantly dwelling on the inevitable. What I'm saying is that if we all address and investigate this truth, we can use what we find *to our advantage in our lives*. How? How can any of this be to our advantage? More on that later, but, in short:

understanding that everything will end helps us appreciate what we have now.

Why I am qualified to write this book, part 1

I'm not.

Well, at least not more than anyone else. Every single one of us will, someday, become an expert on death: what it means when it's someone else's time, and what it means when it's ours.

So I'm not anyone special. But I have given this subject a lot of energy, and if you're reading this now, you could maybe use a friend like me. This whole thing I'm doing by writing this book is about growing together. I want to share what I've learned about making peace with death. I want to encourage you to go deeper. And I want to know what *you've* learned too (I mean it! Contact information is at facebook.com/miguelgilbertchen). Then we can use what we find to help still other people.

Why I am qualified to write this book, part 2

As a child, I never really thought much about death. I had two loving parents, an awesome older sister, some close friends. It never occurred to me that these people might not always be there. My days were spent thinking about kid stuff, like comic books or going on adventures. If something unpleasant happened, it usually wouldn't matter even by the end of that very same day. Kids are cool that way, unattached and pretty much living one moment at a time.

We used to go to church when I was really little. Over time, my family shifted away from organized religion and more toward spirituality, but maybe that's neither here nor there.

I don't remember much about church besides not really liking it. I do however remember a priest. His name is lost to me, but I recall he was a happy person who genuinely seemed to care for his community. I think I took it for granted: *Go to church, see the friendly priest. Repeat.*

Then—you guessed it—all of a sudden he wasn't there anymore. It's a very faint memory, but it's perhaps the first time I became aware that people I knew could die.

My next few encounters were pretty textbook: dead guinea pig, dead family dog. I had a grandfather I knew was dead, but whom I couldn't remember.

These things all made me sad, sure, but they weren't going to derail my entire existence. I still had two loving parents, my awesome older sister Ana, and my close friends. All these people had always been there, and as far as I could tell, they would continue to be. I hadn't yet really felt death's deep impact. Boy howdy, was that all about to change.

I was a teenager. My parents sat my sister and me down in the living room. Mom was sick, they explained.

No big deal, I thought—everyone got sick, I got sick, and everyone got better. But this sickness was different, they told me, and it had a name. An awful, evil, heartbreaking fucking name: *Cancer.* My mother was dying.

I would try as hard as I could to avoid that fact, but in the end I would fail miserably. Death, this time, absolutely *demanded* my attention.

The months after my mother's death were, naturally, a very trying time for the sixteen-year-old me. My *friends* all still had moms, why couldn't *I* have a mom? And it was devastating to see my father and my sister hurting, and hurting so much. Mom had been the backbone of our family; how were we supposed to go forward without her?

We did our best, supporting each other all we could and trying to go on living normal lives, whatever that meant.

This death stuff hurt more than anything I had ever experienced. So far.

Now we jump ahead to seven months after my mom died. My father was out of the country on business. It was the first time since Mom had passed that he actually felt okay enough to go on a trip. He didn't want to leave Ana and me, but it was only a few days that he'd be gone, and we assured him we'd be okay. It would end up being the last time the three of us would be together.

Every year on July 4, Laramie, Wyoming (like nearly every little town in the USA) has a sort of festival. There's music, games, food; the whole community comes together. In 2002, my punk band somehow wormed our way into the festivities. My sister came to watch us play in front of a crowd of *supremely* bummed-out families, all just trying to enjoy their holiday without a bunch of green- and blue-haired weirdos who weren't old enough to vote screaming about the fucked-up state of politics. (Some things never change.) After our set, Ana came up, said she enjoyed it, and that she'd see me at home later.

I went off riding bikes with my friends, getting in the usual trouble, and by the time I came home, she was asleep. In the morning I woke up to a note from her saying she'd gone shopping in Fort Collins, Colorado, with a couple of friends. I thought nothing of it and went on with my day. That night, though, I received a phone call.

There had been an accident.

Things go through your head at a moment like that.

Desperation.

Denial.

Prayer.

But none of it could change the news this call dropped on me. My sister was dead. The car she'd been in turned onto Highway 287 and was T-boned by another car. Her friend was in a coma and the other passenger had broken both legs. Ana had died instantly.

You'll recall that my father was out of the country. Imagine having to tell *anyone* that their baby girl was dead at age 20. Imagine having to tell them that just months after their partner had passed away. Now imagine it's your own father.

And Ana had been "the good one"—or at least that's how I thought of it. *I* was the fuck-up. I wanted nothing more than for it to have been me instead.

I began a downward spiral to the darkest, most hopeless place I would ever encounter.

Those deaths were devastating.
But there was more to come.

Death doesn't stop. It's been my constant companion since I was 16. Over the years, I would lose friends, more relatives, bandmates. More recently, my band Teenage Bottlerocket lost our drummer, best friend, and brother, Brandon Carlisle.

And, yes, things got really fucking dark for me.

But things also got really fucking *beautiful*. I heard it said once that death can either break you or break your heart wide open. I think it's a little of both. When we start facing the truth instead of running away, though, we get stronger and more open-hearted than ever. If we can face death, arguably we can face any challenges that come our way. We can find out that we are stronger than we've previously believed.

So yeah, I'm just another person who has been affected by death, another person who will someday be dead. Hardly special.

But if I, the fuck-up, can make peace with loss—and even flourish in ways because of it—then anyone can.

This means you, my friend.

Let's go there.

3

It Happens to Everyone

Death is not waiting for us at the end of the road. It is walking with us the whole time. —LARRY ROSENBERG

LITERALLY EVERY SINGLE person who has ever lived has died or will someday. An obvious enough statement—and yet we pretend it isn't, and our pretending isn't helping anyone. To say we, as a society, are uncomfortable with the thought of death is a massive understatement. To say that death is humankind's greatest fear might be closer to the truth.

Usually, we try to ignore it. We distract ourselves, focusing on literally anything else. Though, I'm guessing that since you're reading this book, you've somehow come to the point where you can no longer ignore death, where ignoring it isn't really working for you anymore. Maybe someone in your life has recently passed away or is near the end.

Maybe you're staring at yourself in the mirror and considering your own mortality.

Neither's easy. We all feel aversion to the subject, even when we're consciously trying to come to grips with it. But it's that aversion—and not death itself—that trips us up. After all, death is just part of life. Always has been. The final part of it, yes, but still: death in and of itself isn't such a bad thing!

It's okay to not want to hear that. Maybe you've lost someone you've loved and suffered deeply for it. That's legit. But before you tell me to fuck off, let's talk about that suffering. Which is not the same thing as *pain*.

Pain and suffering (Sounds fun, doesn't it? Read on!)

Me, I've found Buddhism helpful in thinking about this stuff. Our friends the Buddhists have a good handle on the difference between pain and suffering. You step on a nail? Pain. You get your toes run over by a skateboard? Pain. Baseball to the privates? Well . . . you get the idea. *Life is full of pain.* (Need a name for your new emo band? You're welcome.)

Life is full of pain, and we really can't escape it. Not only that, but the more we try to escape the inescapable, the more we'll suffer! But, from this same perspective, suffering can be seen as an optional companion to pain. For example: say you broke your arm. It hurt when that happened. That's pain. Now, say you sit around, bummed as fuck that you have a broken arm. Your day/week/month is ruined because of it. Every time you look at your cast you're reminded that you probably shouldn't have front-flipped off the roof onto that trampoline, and now you feel like a total idiot. A total idiot with a broken arm. But the actual pain of the arm breaking was over with long ago, and still you choose to continue feeling bad. That is suffering.

You can't change the fact that your arm is broken, but you *can* choose to stop amplifying your suffering about it.

Like your busted-ass arm, there are other things that can't be changed. Death is definitely one of them. Now, I'm not being cold in a *"Yeah, people die, get over it"* kind of way. What I'm trying to say is that there's a healthy way for us to feel the pain we need to feel—and also move forward. Which brings us to . . .

Clinging and aversion

From the Buddhists' perspective, we suffer because we are fighting an impossible fight against the truth, pushing against reality to make it something other than what it is. We try to hold on to things that are seemingly pleasurable (clinging) and push away things that are seemingly unpleasant (aversion). This pattern of clinging and aversion causes us to be disconnected from reality, and failing to see that, we keep pushing, making the disconnection worse. That disconnect is true suffering.

Of course, it's not only the Buddhists who've understood this. If you're from a Christian background (or are a *Seinfeld* fan), you're probably aware of the idea of *serenity*. The famed "Serenity Prayer" goes:

God, grant me the serenity to accept the things
    I cannot change,

Courage to change the things I can,
And wisdom to know the difference.

Questions about God aside, the sentiment here is right on the money: there are things we can change, and things we cannot, and the more we can accept all that—the more we can let go of our clinging and aversion—the less we will suffer.

Easy enough when talking about a broken arm or a bad song on the radio, but *death*? *Eesh.* Not so easy. So how do we stop *clinging* to life? How do we let go of our aversion to death?

We practice making and taking the time to investigate the things we're afraid of, to connect with the truth of death, and to allow ourselves to be present with it. It's not always easy, but it can help us deeply.

A middle way

Now, we don't *personally* know what dying is like, but we do know that, from a physical standpoint at least, being alive and being dead are pretty different. You can call a living friend on the phone or pop by their house to visit. You cannot do that with your dead grandparent. (You can try, I guess, but it will be very different than when they were alive. I'm betting. And if their phone number has since been given to someone else, you will have a very confused stranger on the line wondering why you're calling them Abuelita.)

Think about someone you love deeply. You wish they could live forever! You could spend your life afraid that they will die, wishing with all your might that they won't, until one day they do. *Or,* you could enjoy the time you are given with them, softly aware that, yes, someday it will be over. I'd rather spend my time present than worrying. And it's totally doable, being present. Worries might still arise, but over time we can get better at letting them go rather than allowing them to overtake us. This is our practice.

Another way to go, on the opposite end of the spectrum, would be to completely ignore the fact that this person you love is going to die someday. A sort of out-of-sight, out-of-mind mentality. Maybe, if you don't think about them dying, they just *won't*! Until they do, and it will be pretty fucking hard to ignore, and you won't be prepared for it at *all.*

But there's a middle way.

In this middle-way scenario, you have *put in time* understanding and exploring the reality of death. You've become reasonably aware of the finite nature of life. Because of this, you are neither compelled to sit around worrying that your loved one will die, nor to take your time together for granted. You know that time is limited and you appreciate it. In a certain sense, this is the absence of clinging and aversion.

This same mentality can be applied even after your loved one has died. At that point the truth becomes that they are gone. You don't get a choice about that. It will hurt. You will undoubtedly experience very real, very profound pain. But it's possible to feel that pain and not cause yourself undue suffering.

Feeling that pain is hard, but it sure beats aversion. I tried the aversion route when my mother and sister died, and I can tell you: it's impossible. You might spend a decade on drugs, desperately trying not to feel the pain, but all you will have done is prolonged it, turning it into real, ongoing suffering.

You won't do much better with clinging. Your loved one will remain very dead, and no amount of wishing and wanting will make the truth untrue.

So we return to the middle.

In the middle, we can *feel* the pain. We can be truly, deeply sad about our loved one's passing. But we can also feel joy. We can have good days. We can move forward in our lives. We can find beauty all around us. We can allow ourselves to be transformed by our pain into something even greater.

This is much easier said than done, of course, and so we must practice for it, taking manageable steps each day so we're not completely blindsided when death does pay us a visit.

How do we start practicing with death?
(Or nearly anything else?)

Sitting still is always a good place to start. We can call this meditation, we can call it just sitting still. Some people talk about it in spiritual or mystical terms; some people just see it as a chance to chill or reset. The basic idea is this:

1. Find someplace quiet if you can. But if you wanna do this on the subway, that's fine too.
2. Sit tall and comfortable, relaxed yet firm.
3. Let your gaze soften or your eyes close.

4. Take a deep breath or two in, and let a deep breath or two out. Let your breath settle and keep breathing naturally.
5. Pay attention in this moment of stillness.

That stillness is the beginning of peace.

A little stillness can go a long way. Let's find a little more.

4

___

PRACTICE:
Here's Your Meditation Foundation

So, SITTING STILL may be really beneficial, but it isn't always super-easy to do. It's one thing to say we're going to sit in stillness; it's another thing to actually do it.

You'll get the chance to try a number of practices in this book, all meant to help us better connect with different ideas about and aspects of death. To make the most of them, it'll help to first establish a foundation we can build on as our journey and practice continue. So let's take the basic approach to practice we ended our last chapter with and deepen it some. Your moment of stillness awaits.

Turn off, tune in

First things first: sitting still is hard enough without a blaring TV, a ringing phone, or a barking dog to distract you.

Turn the TV off! Leave your phone somewhere else! Put the dog outside or give her a rawhide. It might not always be possible to find complete silence: You might have noisy roommates or neighbors, or live next to a loud-ass train station. That's okay, remove any distractions you can, soften the others, and as best you can allow them to become white noise.

Then, find as quiet a space as possible. It can be useful, though not necessary, to keep a timer nearby. If your timer happens to be on your phone, well, at least put the damned thing in airplane mode!

Use your butt

Now, a big part of sitting still is *sitting*. We've all presumably got butts—time to put them to use. Some teachers will suggest you sit in a very specific manner, on a cushion or blanket, legs crossed or sitting on your knees, or what-have-you. I'm not going to be so specific. You can sit on a chair, or a cushion, or wherever. There are just two important factors I'd like for you to keep in mind:

First, however you choose to sit, be reasonably comfortable. Not "I'm gonna fall asleep in my favorite recliner" comfortable, but at least "I can sit here for a while without feeling like my legs are gonna fall off" comfortable. Some might argue that working through the pain of first taking up sitting without moving is part of meditation practice, and I'd ultimately agree with them. But not for our purposes in this book. We've got bigger fish to fry, so let's take physical discomfort out of the equation as much as reasonably possible and free our energy up for other pursuits. Sounds good, right?

Next: however you choose to sit, try to be consistent. Practices seem to go better when consistency is applied. If you practice once a month for two hours, you won't really notice any improvement. But if you practice most days for even five minutes, that consistency will help you make note of how the practice feels, and how it changes, over time.

Okay. So I'm sitting. Now what?

So here you are, sitting, in a quiet room. If you're using a timer, you'll want to set it for your desired amount of time. I'd say start with 5–10 minutes. That'll be enough for now.

Let's check your posture and start meditating, step by step.

1. Check your posture. Find a tall, but relaxed, spine. Roll your shoulders away from your ears. Take any last wiggles or movements you need to be comfortable, and then sit still. Let your gaze soften, and if more comfortable than not, close your eyes.
2. Take a couple deep breaths in and out and then just let your breath settle. Just breathe naturally. You don't have to do anything special.
3. Start noticing your breath. Notice that you are breathing in. Notice the sensation of the air as it moves in your nostrils and expands into your lungs. Notice the brief pause at the top of your inhalation. Now, exhale. Notice that you are breathing out. Notice the sensation of the air as it empties from your lungs and out your nostrils. Notice the short, natural pause at the end of your exhalation. Again.
4. Continue. Take a mindful breath in, a mindful pause,

and let a mindful breath out. "Mindful" can simply mean noticing completely; in this case, noticing each part of your breath. This is the foundation of our practice. It seems simple on paper, but there is more to it than initially meets the eye. Keep breathing this way until your timer dings.

You might notice that the mind begins to wander. This is natural. Our minds have a tendency—you could even say they're *conditioned*—to avoid stillness. Try to be skillful here, avoiding judging yourself for how your meditation time goes. If we're trying to cultivate some amount of stillness, distracting thoughts can be a source of great frustration. Sure. But getting frustrated and angry won't get us any closer to stillness. Quite the opposite: the more we get frustrated and try to force ourselves not to think, the more we will think at a million-thoughts-an-hour.

So what can we do?

First and foremost, remember: you are doing something nice for yourself. This is not an unkind practice, so don't be unkind to yourself. Try to maintain a playful attitude. (Some people find that meditating with an "inward smile" on your face—one you can feel, but that others wouldn't perceive—can help with that.) If you're being kind to yourself, you can work with distractions without stressing about them.

So if you notice (and maybe even give chase to) a distracting thought as you're breathing, just acknowledge it. You can have a little fun with it at first, even. Perhaps feel that inward smile a little more, or say to yourself, "A-ha!"

But *then* get back to business and formalize what you've noticed. Replace what you've noticed with the simple thought, "I'm thinking." Once you've acknowledged the thought, then as best you can, breathe with it, and let it go with an exhalation. And just resume your noticing of your in- and out-breaths.

The distractions that come up during your meditation might come up once or twice. They might come up a million freaking times. It's all the same. Just notice you've been distracted, acknowledge it, and return. If you can access a playful attitude through the duration of your practice time, that's good.

Practices to come later in the book will ask you to refer to this foundation as your starting point. (Again: consistency will help. A lot.) So get familiar with this very basic practice. It'll be useful all the way to The End.

5

Heaven

I was thinking about how people seem to read the Bible a lot more as they get older, and then it dawned on me—they're cramming for their final exam. —GEORGE CARLIN

Scenario time!

It's a normal Tuesday, like a million other Tuesdays you've had before. You're walking down the street, doing normal Tuesday stuff. Unbeknownst to you, just down the street a disaster is waiting to happen. Let's say for some reason (maybe a surprise birthday party for some rich CEO?), an elephant needs to be lifted up to the twentieth story of a building. Let's also say the people in charge of getting said elephant lifted are not trained and licensed elephant-lifters—and thus have no idea what they're doing.

Well, they're about to have a big lawsuit and a bigger mess on their hands. Because, here you come, walking your normal Tuesday shoes down the normal Tuesday street when suddenly . . . *SPLAT!* Four tons of elephant fall on your head out of freaking nowhere. You die instantly.

The elephant is fine. (What do you think I am in this thought-experiment, some kind of monster?) But you're not fine. You're toast.

Your smooshed body isn't going to be of much use anymore, so it's time to leave that, this planet, and this life behind. The lights, as they say, go out . . .

But then a new light comes on. You feel an irresistible urge to head toward it. It's a comforting feeling, one of coming home.

A quick Google search will tell you that many who have had near-death experiences report seeing this bright light. Of course, another quick Google search will tell you that some scientists believe it to be a delusion caused by lack of oxygen to the brain, but for our purposes, let's say this light is the real deal. You're going to heaven. FUCK, YES! Follow that light!

But then what? Will you float around in some beautiful clouds? Will all of your dreams come true? Is your childhood dog, Mr. Willem Dafoe, going to run up and lick you any second now? Heaven means a lot of things to a lot of people.

For some, it might mean sitting in the presence of their God. You know: angels, harps, basking in their maker's glory in a state of pure bliss for all eternity. For others, heaven doesn't necessarily imply the existence of God; it merely means a sort of perfection: a place, a state, where suffering has ceased. Some religions speak of a more literal paradise where the righteous are rewarded greatly.

I like to think that heaven is beyond our human wants. (My idea of heaven is probably very different from yours, but perhaps we can at least agree that heaven is *perfect*. If it wasn't perfect, it wouldn't really be heaven, now would it?) Sure, endless taco buffets and puppy parties might seem like a cool way to spend eternity, but even that could get old after a while. Heaven, to be truly worth spending eternity in, would have to go deeper.

In our human lives, we want a lot: cars, houses, cool jobs, money, tacos, exciting trips, a bajillion dollars . . . Nothing wrong with any of that—as long as we're not lost in attachment. More on this later.

I don't have a bajillion dollars and presumably never will. That's okay. I have a fulfilling life anyway. And while my experiences have made life a pretty sweet ride so far, I could have had a completely different set of experiences and it might have been equally amazing. If we're not attached, our wants aren't necessarily problematic. We have to work to know the difference between what we want and what we need to be happy.

If we really look at our existence, we might argue that the only thing we really need (beyond having our basic biological needs met) is to feel love, in one form or another. Not a fearful, fragile love but a pure, unbreakable love. Do you really *need* a fancy new car, or a flashy new job, if you have a heart full of love? We might feel this love for our children, or for our partner, or we might even be lucky enough to feel pure love for ourselves from time to time. This type of love brings joy, regardless of our other wants. Maybe that type of love is what heaven is really all about.

• • • • •

Okay, back to our elephant scenario. You'll recall that you've been squished out of existence, and now you're following a white light to heaven.

So what do you see when you get there? Maybe you see God. Maybe your version of heaven isn't reliant on God. Either is fine; this is *your* idea of perfection, remember?

Maybe in heaven, we'd be fully free from want and attachment. No suffering, just deep, fulfilling love. That's the kind of heaven I hope my loved ones would find. Speaking of loved ones: *Are* your deceased loved ones waiting there for you with open arms? It's a comforting thought, isn't it? And one I believe goes with all versions of heaven. Or at least should, imho.

Hmm. Maybe we've actually hit a little snag here, with this version of heaven. I mean, what if your loved ones weren't exactly saintly? In many traditions, and particularly the Christian religions, the paradise/afterlife is reserved for those who have lived what are deemed to be righteous lives. Not righteous like a sick guitar solo, but righteous meaning living by a set of moral and social disciplines outlined in a particular faith's rulebook. This can be problematic for a few different reasons.

First, there are *a lot* of different rulebooks, and they don't agree on a lot of things. How in heaven's name (snare hit/ cymbal crash) are we supposed to know which rulebook is right? (By process of elimination, we can narrow things down. For example, in my opinion, any of the rulebooks that say homosexuality is a sin can fuck right off. I'm more about the rulebooks that tell us to love everyone.) Maybe the "right" rulebook is a really weird, obscure one where we all have to wear pants on our heads and eat Spaghetti-O's every other Tuesday. Who knows?

(No one *knows*.)

For argument's sake, let's say we *do* know which rulebook is the correct one, we follow it to a T, and we *are* going to heaven. The theory is still problematic. What if Mom didn't follow the rulebook? What if she was a loving, kind, amazing person, but she didn't wear the pants-hat or eat the Spaghetti-O's? If she doesn't get in, but you do, doesn't that ruin *your* heaven? . . . Especially if she went to The Other Place (which we will visit next). Hardly sounds "perfect" to me.

Still, there are many beautiful things about the heaven theory, and we might even find some practical place for it in our day-to-day lives. For example, the promise of an eternity of bliss can be a great motivator. The ideal of heaven can be a good reminder to try our best.

It can also help us heal. If we have lost someone close to us, it can be comforting to believe (or even just imagine) that they still exist *somewhere*. It can bring us some peace to think of our loved ones as safe, at peace and waiting for us in a better place.

And heaven can help us find the beauty in daily life. Maybe we all experience moments of heaven periodically. As I look at my baby daughter's eyes, even at 3 in the morning for a diaper change, there is no doubt in my heart that perfect moments exist. So is that a little heaven, here and now? I say it is. I'm sure you've had at least one moment like that in your life, even if it seems like a distant memory. And if you've had one perfect moment, you can have another. As our friend Belinda Carlisle (a Buddhist, by the way) sang, *"Oooh, heaven is a place on earth."*

Before we move to The Other Place, let's take some time for a quick practice, to try and connect to and reflect on the idea of heaven.

6

PRACTICE:

A Moment of Heaven

Step 1: Download and listen to Belinda Carlisle's *Heaven Is a Place on Earth*. (Just kidding.) (But not really. That song is a fucking *jam*.)

For real though, here's our practice:

1. Grab a pen and some paper.
2. Find somewhere quiet, free from distraction. Spend a few moments breathing, clearing your mind, and creating space.
3. Take 5–10 minutes and write out any thoughts you have about what heaven might look like. I'll avoid giving too many more cues, because I don't want to further influence your answers. Just think about what your idea of heaven would look like. There are no right or wrong

answers, just whatever feels like it would be *the* perfect place to spend eternity.

4. When you've finished writing, take a moment to look back over your words, then sit in silence with them for a few moments. Let yourself feel whatever comes up.

I'd love to hear about your ideas of what heaven could be. Share it at facebook.com/miguelgilbertochen (That is, unless your heaven is a place where Facebook doesn't exist. Which it probably should be. And speaking of Facebook, we're gonna talk about hell now.)

7

Hell

Death is when the monsters get you.   —STEPHEN KING

THINKING ABOUT HEAVEN . . . that was nice, right? But as they say, you can't have the light without the dark; *ipso facto*, if we entertain the idea of heaven, we must also explore its opposite. Let's strap on our studded black leather, pump some Judas Priest, and explore The Fiery Pits of Hell.

Most of the major religions that believe in heaven also believe in some kind of hell. No reward for a life well lived, hell is heaven's opposite. Instead of clouds and angels, hell is associated with fire, *El Diablo*, and/or endless suffering beyond imagination.

What exactly does "endless suffering beyond imagination" mean? Does it mean burning and torture at the hands of demons; fingernails pried off one by one and skin removed with a potato peeler? Do you get a paper cut in between your toes, then it heals and someone gives you a fresh one again? Does hell mean 24/7 Smashmouth's "All-Star" at full volume on eternal repeat?

I imagine there are people out there who wouldn't mind listening to Smashmouth. [*Shiver.*] I also imagine there are people who have known great suffering already, for whom the idea of eternal paper cuts doesn't actually seem so frightening. Which brings me to some sort of point about hell: it has to be really personal. Just as one person's vision of heaven might fall short for another, hell can only be effective if it's *tailored to the individual.*

For example, I'm crazy allergic to cats. I don't have anything against cats, I just get really sneezy, itchy, and short of breath if I'm around them for too long. In my version of heaven, there are lots and lots of happy dogs. (There can be cats too, but somehow I'm not allergic to them.) In my hell, though, there are cats *everywhere* and I have no medication and even though I wanna pet them and make friends, I can't because I can't breathe. My *real* version of hell would probably a lot more fucked-up than that, but you get the point. Someone else might go to Miguel's Cat Hell and find themselves in their own Cat Heaven. So if Satan or whoever in hell is in charge wanted to punish us both, he'd have to put me in Cat Hell and the other person in some unimaginable (to them at least) catless void.

Or let's instead consider something we can all agree is to be avoided. How about . . . being repeatedly stabbed and burned for all eternity? Well, as I said before, some notion of physical pain might not be a big deal compared to what we actually experience in life. (Plus, can we even feel physical pain if we've died? Doesn't shedding our physical body imply also shedding physical sensations? But I digress.) The point is: hell has to be deeper than our *surface* fears.

Let's, for a moment, go back to heaven. If you're in heaven, have the endless-taco-bar, perfect-weather, hanging-with-God existence, but one of your most beloved family members is missing . . . well, that's not *heaven*. On the opposite side of the same coin, what if you're in hell—burn-and-stab central HQ—but at the end of each torture session, you get to spend a few minutes with all of your loved ones? Which scenario would you take? Can all of the "heavenly" stuff imaginable ever mean anything if you're without the people you love? And don't we find that even the most hellish periods of our lives are made at least tolerable thanks to the presence and support of loved ones? The line between heaven and hell can get pretty blurry—and that's all down to love.

You see, just as any place and any moment can feel like heaven if you're filled with love, anywhere can be hell if you're without it. I've heard it said that hell is the absence of God, and I always found this to be an interesting depiction. In this version of hell, there is no fire or brimstone, no paper cuts or pitchforks. There is also no God, and depending on your background, that might seem like a good, bad, or neutral thing.

Which brings me to my next question: can hell exist without God or the devil?

Now, there are those who live their entire lives based on what they think God wants from them, trying to avoid spending eternity with the devil. If you fall in that category, okay. I'm certainly not here to argue against what works for you. Perhaps some will argue that fear of hell can make us live better lives. If you don't happen to see things that way (a lot of us don't), I think that's okay too. We're all just working with what we've got and doing our best. Now, let's say our best falls short, and we are off to hell to be punished. Just who is it who's punishing us? I can't get behind the idea of a God who would let us burn forever.

We've probably all heard at one point or another that God is love. Looking at that through an abstract lens, we come a little closer to an idea of God that I think works universally, or at least works better than the idea of a bearded dude on a cloud giving us all the thumbs-up or thumbs-down. Regardless of religious background or lack thereof, I think many of us can agree that a huge difference between heaven and hell—or at least heavenliness and hellishness—would be the presence or absence of love. Just as the taco bar without love would be hell, a world where Smashmouth plays 24/7 could still be heaven if it was also infused with love.

Let's take this a step further. Let's say that we all inherently have love inside us. We don't need to be given anything to *feel* it; it just resides in us at our most basic level. Furthermore, this inherent love can never be taken from us. If you've had a loved one die, you might be familiar with the feeling that their love for you still continues, as yours does for them. Nothing can take that away, though of course you can feel a huge disconnect from it sometimes. Being disconnected from love? That feels like punishment. And whether it's God or you yourself inflicting this punishment, it's hellish. You don't even have to die to feel it.

Now's a good time to recall our friends the Buddhists and their thoughts about pain versus suffering. Pain, as they see it, is the inevitable, real part of being a human; suffering is our unskillful reaction to that pain. We *can* stub our toe and feel pain, but not suffer about it. Likewise, I would say that the human spirit is so powerful that we could be burning in hell, feeling a constant influx of pain, and still find a way to not suffer. And if you're not suffering, then in a way, you're not in hell.

There are varying ideas about whether hell is eternal or a place you go to repent, then eventually transcend. I prefer the latter idea. Remove the eternal damnation and the classical model of heaven and hell becomes palatable again: if you'd been sent *upstairs*, and your mom was *downstairs*, you could know the separation was only temporary. You could see hell as a healing process, albeit a painful and dark one. Once a person had gone through hell, they might be reconnected to their deepest self, one that knew only love, and at that point they could make it to heaven. And if you had been in heaven without them, your lesson would simply be patience, knowing that when they were ready, your loved ones would join you.

Me, I love this idea of hell as a healing process because it can be applied to how we look at things day to day while we're alive. We feel a lot of pain, and very often we suffer. When we suffer we are in hell, no matter if it looks like Kuai or a fiery pit. But this hell is temporary; there is a way out. If we can create hell in our own lives, then we can also create heaven.

8

PRACTICE:

What the Hell?

LET'S SIT WITH the possible practical benefits of the (supposed) existence of hell. As with all the practices in this book and *I Wanna Be Well*, I'll encourage you to begin with a few minutes of quiet breathing. (You may want to refer to the "Meditation Foundation" instructions on page 21.) And you'll want to have pen and paper nearby.

1. Find your distraction-free place, sit comfortably, and breathe.
2. After a few minutes, spend some time writing in response to the following questions. Remember, there are no wrong or right answers; just exploration.

  • What would my own personal hell look like? *Warning: this can be an extremely challenging practice. You might start by dipping your toes into this question rather than going straight for the deep end. Take manageable steps, and each time you practice try to go a little deeper.*

- Can fear of hell make us better people?
- Should it?

If you come up with anything particularly interesting, send it to me in hell—I mean, on Facebook—at facebook.com/miguelgilbertochen.

9

The In-Between

We all wonder about death, where people go and what happens. But certainly, they cross over from this dimension to another one.
—DOLORES O'RIORDAN

SOME RELIGIONS HOLD that there's not just heaven and hell, but a place in between. Some religions even believe there are several such places, where—depending on your *life*—you will spend part of your *after*life. You've heard about limbo and purgatory, but maybe you've never paid them much mind. After all, aren't they each just some sort of pit stop on the way to your final destination, whatever that may be?

But let's pay them a little mind now, starting with limbo. It sure *sounds* like the funner of the two, doesn't it?

Baby Limbo and Heathen Adult Limbo

Fun or not—(hint: *not fun at all*)—limbo was still a widely accepted idea back when I was growing up in the Catholic Church. (My family and I have long since left.) The Basic Limbo Idea was that it was where the unbaptized went. So, not hell, but also not heaven. Heaven, you see, was reserved for those who had picked the right rulebook (or had it picked for them).

There were even two different areas in limbo for the unbaptized. One was reserved for adults who had chosen not to be baptized and thus wouldn't have been "saved" before they died. *Harsh.* But not as harsh as Limbo #2. That's where babies and children who'd not had a chance to be baptized would go. The logic was that, since it wasn't their choice, they shouldn't be punished as harshly as the adults who had consciously chosen not to be baptized. Still, rules were rules, and if you weren't baptized, you couldn't get into heaven. (Thanks, Mom and Dad!)

Eventually, the Catholic Church caught up to the rest of the world and decided that an innocent baby being excluded from heaven through no fault of their own was, well, shitty. (The papal decree using the word "shitty" seems to be lost to the sands of time.) So in 2007, the Church updated its rulebook by deleting both Baby Limbo and Heathen Adult Limbo.

Purgatory

Okay so limbo is *so, totally, over.* But purgatory remains. And just as limbo sounds like it maybe isn't so bad, purgatory sounds really heavy but is kinda Nowheresville. Literally: purgatory isn't quite life, and it's not quite heaven or hell, either. It's the great in-between, and some say it represents a second chance. Where limbo turned out to be more of a destination, purgatory's really more a pit stop. Let's check it out. No dying needed.

Scenario time: Limbo vs. Purgatory, round 1

Let's say, for scenario's sake at least, that you're a pretty good person. (Chances are that's true, even if it doesn't *always* seem that way.) You're not perfect, but you're trying your best in life. (Also quite possibly true!) Let's also say that your company hosts a yearly Christmas party, and the festivities include doing the limbo, the well-known group event where dancers take turns passing under an increasingly lowering stick, trying not to touch it. (I'm sorry for the obvious *limbo* scenario, I couldn't help myself. But limbo has origins in Trinidad as a ritual during wakes or funerals, which for whatever reason speaks to me as I'm working out this scenario.)

Anyhoo, *it's Limbo time!* You and your coworkers have had a couple extra eggnogs and are taking turns dancing under the limbo stick. Everyone's having a blast. It's your turn when the unexpected happens: a giant fucking elephant falls through the roof and squashes you under the limbo stick. As before, the result of the falling elephant is, of course, that she's fine, you're dead, and your coworkers are in shock. Also, the elephant-lifting people are starting to realize that maybe they're not cut out for this line of work.

Now, as I say, you're dead but were a pretty good person, so you're not going to hell. Then again, your record wasn't exactly squeaky clean either. A few minor sins here and there can really add up. So you're not headed to heaven either. At least not yet. Enter purgatory. (See what I mean about it sounding heavy? *Enter purgatory* is so metal. *Enter limbo*, not so much.)

Dante Alighieri's *Divine Comedy*, which comprises his works *Inferno*, *Purgatorio*, and *Paradiso*, is not just some of the most important literature of the Middle Ages; it is largely responsible for how we think of purgatory. There are, famously, nine levels, each corresponding to an obstacle to heaven: stubbornness, lack of repentance, wrath, envy, pride, sloth, lust, gluttony, and greed. Were you a prideful or greedy jerk? Well, now you know where you'll end up—for at least a little while.

But you'll hardly be alone. Most of us have committed one or more of those so-called deadly sins at various points of our lives. (Some of us may have banged most of them out before our morning commute!) Our job is to recognize our wrongs and make them right. Whether we do that while we're still breathing or not will dictate where we end up. Or so it's said.

Now, I'm not here to argue what is and isn't a sin. (I'll say again that being gay, lesbian, or bi- or any other non-binary designation is NOT. Period.) We may all have different mores and morals, but I think we can agree that some things are just wrong. For example: murder. You shouldn't be murdering people. Or drop-kicking puppies. Don't do that.

As for overeating or being lazy or overly prideful? Well, there's room for debate there, right? Some say these "deadly sins" will delay or possibly deny you your entry into heaven. Others might say you're just being lazy, eating too much, or your head's gotten a little big. Let's just say some things can land you in between heaven and hell, with an extra workload to take care of before you can move on.

Moving on is the key idea here. In purgatory, you get another chance to make up for your wrongdoings. Maybe you need to make amends with people you hurt in life, maybe you need to repent to God or help others avoid making the same mistakes you did. I'm not sure how you're meant to make up for your wrongdoings, but the idea is once you've done so, you can move on. This is good news for us humans, being that we have a tendency to procrastinate and not face up to our misdeeds. Too often we die with unfinished business.

Scenario time: Limbo vs. Purgatory, round 2

In this case (and again, probably in real life) you were a pretty good person, or at least you tried to be. However, a few months before the fateful Christmas party, you *committed a sin*. Let's say your sister and you got in a huge fight, you lost your temper, used a bunch of swearwords; we're going to consider this blowing your stack and cursing a sin. You felt bad about the argument afterward and kept hoping you and your sister would make amends. But she never apologized for her part of the fight, and so neither did you. You both put it off, thinking that when the time was right you would set things straight again. It never happened, and now you're basically a human-shaped tattoo on an elephant's ass.

If we accept that you have sinned, and we accept the idea of heaven and hell, then we must also accept that your sin could keep you out of heaven. Does that seem fair? Should you, the angry, swearword-slinging sinner, end up in hell, same as Adolf Hitler or Jeffrey Dahmer, never to be allowed into heaven? Of course not! Thanks to purgatory, you still have another chance to make things right and end up on that taco bar in the clouds with all your loved ones. All you have to do is cleanse, purify, and atone for your sins. But what in purgatory does *that* even mean?

Atonement can be thought of as admitting our wrongs and doing what we can to reverse them. But it really means owning our actions, being at one with them. (Think of it as *at-one-ment*.) Being at one with our actions means being responsible for them, which is, of course, easier said than done, at least in the human realm. Perhaps in purgatory it becomes a little easier to take responsibility, because we have been given a second chance. Purgatory allows us to see the nature of our wrongdoings, and it allows us a way out of their shadow. Furthermore, in the afterlife, with our human concerns out of the way, atonement can become our one and only focus. Purgatory becomes less of *a place* and more of *a process*. Think about it: if you didn't have to work a day job, you'd have a lot more time to make amends, wouldn't you?

But to whom are we making amends, and what for exactly?

Some, or at least their "rulebooks," would say it's God who we must make things right with. If that works for you, cool. If that doesn't work for you—and there are more of such people than ever before (atheists, agnostics, people who identify as "spiritual but not religious")—you can still find some value in both purgatory and the idea of atonement if you think of sin not as an act against God, but rather an act of *separation*.

In a perfect world, one where we all love each other and all that stuff, we would all sense that we are deeply connected. There, just as in the world we have now, when we cause some kind of harm, we create a separation, and separation is inherently painful. We should avoid causing harm, not because God will get mad and not let us into heaven, but because of the separation and attendant pain we'd be causing to others and ourselves. Atonement is the *undoing* of this separation, returning things to their harmonious, connected state. (Again, you don't need to believe in literal heaven or purgatory for atoning to work. Try it and see.)

In purgatory, we are given a chance after death to again become *at one* with whatever it is we've become separated from, be it the universe, God, our human and animal brothers and sisters, or even parts of ourselves. When we have *become* one with that which our sin has separated us from, that's when heaven is within our grasp. This means that if purgatory exists, then it's never too late to clean our slate and end up in heaven. It could be argued that this is true, purgatory or not. As long as we're alive we can heal our past misdeeds, and in the purgatory scenario we can do so even after we've passed on. This is a particularly comforting thought when it comes to our loved ones who may have not led lives that would bring them to the pearly gates. Maybe they went by the wrong rulebook, or maybe they had some fuck-ups they never quite made up or atoned for. Thanks to purgatory you can still someday meet them in paradise.

I've lost too many friends to suicide, and it's hard to shake the ingrained idea that what they've done is a great, unforgivable sin; one that we're told will keep them barred from entry into heaven. But, if we take purgatory into account, we can see that nothing is unforgivable. There is always a second chance.

Some believe that the prayers of the living can help those in purgatory move forward into the next stage of the afterlife. I can't know if that's true or not, but I find it comforting, so I pray. Here's a prayer for them, and for us all:

> May our loved ones find their way out of separation and return to at-one-ness. And may those of us still on this earth use our time wisely, recognizing and accepting responsibility for our wrongdoings, and making things right whenever and however we can.

10

Rebirth

I don't believe in reincarnation, and I didn't believe in it when I was a hamster.
                                                    —SHANE RITCHIE

LET'S THINK OUTSIDE the Western/Christian box and explore a completely different take on what happens when we die. Favored among Buddhists, Hindus, and Colorado New Agers, it's—*how'd you guess*?—rebirth and/or reincarnation.

The idea is pretty much as old as civilization. It shows up in ancient Hindu, Buddhist, and even Egyptian texts. The basic idea is that what we do in this life will directly affect how we're born in the next. Total fucking jerk? You might be reborn as a turd or some kind of icky swamp creature. Kind and helpful to others? Maybe you'll find new life as as a well-cared-for puppy or as a human again, but with better circumstances. If you're really, really good, you might even make it past the human realm and be reborn into some higher state. Whoa!

The way the Buddhists think of it is (more or less) that we exist in a cycle of birth, death, and rebirth known as *samsara*. As we long as we remain bound by this cycle, we'll experience some level of suffering. You'll recall from earlier that *pain* is inevitable, but *suffering* is optional. Providing that that's true, then perhaps our ultimate (and arguably doable) goal would be, and should be, to get free from suffering.

Achievement of that goal requires that we must get free from the birth/death/rebirth cycle itself. In the Buddhists' view, death alone doesn't mean the end of our suffering—unlike in some religions, where you can die, go to heaven, and be pain-and-worry free, stylin' on a cloud. In fact, depending on the type of life you lived, death, some Buddhists say, might bring with it a next existence that will be *chock-full-o* suffering.

I know earlier I suggested you could be reborn as a turd. I made that up. There is no "Turd Realm" you might end up in. (Though that *is* an excellent band name.) There is, however, plenty of opportunity to suffer in other rebirth-related ways. You could still end up as an icky swamp lizard or, worse yet, find yourself in one of the many dreaded hell realms. Buddhism's six realms, in order from the least fortunate (shittiest) to the most fortunate (raddest) are: hell, animal, hungry ghost, human, *asura*, and heaven. Which one will you end up in? And just as important, are you already in one now?

1. The **hell realm** (*also* a good band name) is a realm of anger, suffering, punishment, endless Smashmouth; all the bad stuff you'd associate with hell. Obviously, you don't want to end up here. But if you do, it's only for a finite amount of time. (Still.) In this version of hell, you can and will move on to another realm eventually—if you do the work to purify your actions, or *karma*.

2. Next up we have the **animal realm**. Here you might be born some kind of fucked-up frog, or you might land a cozier life, as a puppy in a loving family. This too will depend on your actions in your previous life. However, even though puppy life might sound pretty good, it's still believed to be a less fortunate incarnation than one in the higher realms. This is because a puppy doesn't have the same capacity (arguably) for insight, ability, or opportunity that we humans do—qualities needed to progress toward ultimate liberation. (And if our progress is slow, that means even more time suffering in the samsara cycle.) Think about how attached and upset an untrained puppy is when their owner leaves for work. They can't understand how things really work, so they might sit around all day, anxiously wondering how we'll possibly survive outside without them. They are stuck and suffering over things they don't understand . . . *Sheesh*. Now I'm sad. Everyone be nice to and train your puppies. Moving along.

3. The **hungry ghost realm** is one of complete dissatisfaction. If you're reborn here, you can expect a feeling of always wanting more and never having enough. If attachment is a root cause of suffering (and it is), you can

bet there's plenty of it here. I like to imagine that Slimer from *Ghostbusters* resides in this realm. He's way hungry, and trying to satisfy that hunger is an obsession that keeps him suffering. So it is for anyone who lands in the hungry ghost realm. Nothing they have can or will ever be enough, until they are able to progress beyond this particular rebirth.

4. Landing in the the **human realm** ("You Are Here"—physically speaking, at least) is considered to be a fortunate rebirth, because of humans' potential for liberation, which is so much higher than in the lower realms. We have the tools and ability to consciously work toward freedom from suffering if we want to. But, of course, being born as a human also has many challenges. We might be born into extreme poverty or with a chronic illness. Or, we might be so blinded by ego that we overlook our chance to live a good life and work toward liberation. The potential for things to go really well, or really poorly, is especially present in a human rebirth.

5. The **asura realm** is also known as the "jealous god" realm. Here, maybe, you are a god of some sort, yet you're not free of your desires, so you still suffer. Imagine that: being a super-powerful god, yet you're jealous of your god-neighbor's cool new god-car. You could probably conjure up your own cool new god-car if you thought of it, but you're too caught up in jealousy. In fact, no amount of power can bring satisfaction to those in the asura realm, but they'll keep looking and missing out on their liberation in the process. This can lead, it's said, to a rebirth in a much lower state and undo any progress made in one's previous lives.

6. Finally, there's the **heaven realm**, but don't be fooled. This isn't heaven like we've talked about before. Yes, there may be a taco bar and other forms of joy and bliss. But it's still part of the samsara cycle, the cycle of suffering. In this version of heaven, we are so busy living it up heaven-style that we lose sight of our true nature. If, at the deepest level of our being, we love and care for others, then we must make that central to our existence. In the heaven realm, we forget all that. We're happy, even though our brothers and sisters still suffer. And since we're all interconnected, a part of us suffers as well.

Something beyond

But there's something beyond these six realms. To achieve it, we clear our past karma, free ourselves from attachment, and leave the samsara cycle in the rearview. How to clear our past karma? Well, it depends on the situation, the individual, and a bunch of other factors. Some basic steps to get us started in any case include identifying our past mistakes, understanding where we are now, and taking responsibility. Start here, and you will be well on your way to liberation, also known as enlightenment, *moksha* (in Hinduism or Jainism), or *nirvana* (in Buddhism). Here we can know everlasting, or at least lasting, true bliss. Some say we can experience this in our lifetime, others say it can only be experienced after death, but—dead or alive—the point is: if we really want to be free from suffering, we have to stop playing the birth/death/rebirth game.

We tend to think about birth and rebirth as a matter of life and death, but it can be seen as a moment-by-moment venture. That's to say, that in this very lifetime, we are born and reborn over and over again, literally moment by moment. That's doubly good news. First, it means that it's never too late for us to change. The person that we have been in the past doesn't need to be the person we are today, or even right now. There's possibility for redemption or at least some kind of clean slate. Second, it lets us consider the six realms as real states or phases in which we may spend time during our day-to-day lives.

A perfect day or a moment of bliss might each be seen as a rebirth in the heaven realm and can very quickly be followed by a taste of pure agony in the hell realm. If we are fighting with addiction, we can be seen as existing in the hungry ghost realm, and when we are fixated on meeting our basic needs, we are in the animal realm. The schematics of rebirth can be overlaid on and applied to our lives.

Whether you believe in some kind of literal reincarnation (some essence or aspect of "you" or your life energy being born into a new physical body) or simply your capacity to reinvent and liberate yourself from the same old patterns that have kept you stuck, the idea that we can be reborn is powerfully helpful, if we let it be.

It helps us grapple with the deaths of others to even consider that we might encounter them sometime, somehow again. Have you ever been in a hospital when a baby is born? They'll play a nursery jingle over the PA to announce the new life. When my best friend Brandon passed away, I heard three such jingles announcing triplets. I don't know if these heralded Brandon's return or not, but just the idea that his big, beautiful soul had some kind of relation to these babies—maybe now to the third power!—softened me some, and that helps us when we're trying to process a fresh loss. And who knows? Maybe someday those triplets will somehow play a role in my daughter's life just like Brandon and his twin brother did in mine.

The idea of rebirth is also powerful because it encourages us to take action in our own lives. If we buy into the idea that it's been our past lives that have landed us here, then we can see that our actions now contribute to the creation of a better future. We can take responsibility for our current situation, and this gives us great power. No one else is in charge of our lives if we accept responsibility.

Now, I know some truly awful things happen in life, and much of it might be something no person could ever ask for. This is particularly true if you've been the victim of a violent crime. I'm not here to say that anyone deserves anything like that. No one does. Bad things happen to good people all the time, and my heart goes out to those who have suffered. However I'd like for us all to consider this: whether or not we've "deserved" something, is it possible we could still find power in accepting some responsibility? Not for what happened, but for refusing to be broken and to grow stronger?

So often, the power to move forward is actually ours. In a very real sense, we can be reborn without having to die. And when we're reborn, either literally or figuratively, we can use the circumstances we've been given to create a better present and future.

So how do we make the best of our current birth?

For starters, we commit to being kind to others. From a strictly literal "samsara" perspective, creating good now will help ensure us a fortunate rebirth later, inching us closer to eventual liberation. But even without that perspective, it's clear that helping others is a good way to bring more joy into our own lives immediately. But it's not just about us here. (It never really is.) If we buy into the idea of an ongoing cycle of deaths and rebirths, then we must also consider what that means for our loved ones. If we're subject to death and rebirth, then so are they.

What if that guy who cut you off in traffic really *was* your beloved mother in another life? What if that cow you're eating for lunch *was* once your best friend Steve? Well, you probably wouldn't scream and flip off traffic-mom-guy, and you wouldn't eat the Steve-Burger. And those could be good outcomes whether reincarnation were true or not.

Rebirth might seem like it's about the future, but it's really about the here and now. There's a common misconception that karma is about punishment and reward, but karma really just means action, and what happens because of that action. Action happens now, not yesterday or tomorrow. And doing the right thing feels good, not just in some future life, but in this very moment. So if we live a life of positive karma, then both the action and the reward happen here and now. Living a life in which we commit to doing the right thing will allow us to die—and, perhaps, be reborn—in peace.

If, in our human lives, we are moving up and down constantly through the levels of rebirth, then we must see the potential in each moment: the potential to improve, and the pitfalls we risk if we don't commit to living better. We can see that none of it is permanent, and so we simply try our best. We can even learn to see each moment, each breath, as a practice in taking in and letting go, or being born and dying, only to be reborn again. Rebirth teaches us that we can always be better, in life or after it.

11

Nothing

Actually watching television and surfing the internet are really excellent practice for being dead. —CHUCK PALAHNIUK

QUICK AFTERLIFE RECAP: Heaven is probably pretty nice. Hell is probably not very nice. Purgatory and rebirth are transitions more than final destinations. But what if there's something else—a place where, when we die, is neither good or bad? What if that something else is nothing at all? What if we simply *cease*?

Not a particularly easy idea to wrap one's head around. But let's see if we can.

A whole lot of nothing

If we can *cease existing*, it is easily inferred that we must have *existed to begin with*. That idea's not hard to follow.

After all, we have bodies, minds, jobs, all manner of stuff, likes and dislikes. If we stub our toe it hurts, if we eat pizza it's delicious . . . It sure seems like such experiences are as real as real could be. But some would argue (and sometimes make shockingly convincing cases) that we don't actually exist.

Life, in that view, is just an illusion. Perhaps we're just figments of someone else's imagination, or virtual beings in some kind of computer simulation—a possibility about which Elon Musk, in 2016, said, "There's a one in billions chance we're in base reality." (Neil deGrasse Tyson puts the odds at about 50/50.) Maybe we don't actually exist, we just think we do?

If this theory were true, seems pretty unlikely we'd ever get to know. So, for now, let's just put it out of our minds and assume we exist, shall we?

If we *do* exist, we must ask, *Who or what* are *we anyway?* We have a body; are we that body? We have a mind; are we that mind? Do we have something intangible, like a soul, and if so, is *that* who we really are? There are endless different views on these questions, some with fairly convincing arguments. I'll leave my own thoughts out of it and just say: regardless of who or what we think we are, a theory of eternal nothingness has some big implications.

First, if we believe the theory, then whoever or whatever we are would probably be intrinsically connected to our physical form: whether we *are* our body or a soul that lives *in* the body, our continued existence would rely upon the functionality of said body. If we are a soul that *isn't* reliant on the body, then we could move on to heaven or hell or wherever else. This cannot be true if we are reduced to nothing upon death. In the nothingness theory, our body stops working, and whatever it is we are goes with it. Whether or not you see your death coming, whether you are smashed by an elephant or die in your sleep, the story ends the same. You stop breathing, the lights go out, and that's the end of you forever.

The very idea of "the end of you" (whatever "you" is) will seem incredibly heavy and tragic for some people. (For others—for example, for those who feel overly burdened or bound by aspects of their identity or circumstance—it might actually seem like a bit of relief.) My knee-jerk reaction to this possibility is deep sadness. Not because *I* will be gone, and the world will forever be robbed of my hilarious antics and general awesomeness. There will always be hilarious and awesome people to replace those who have passed. Rather, the idea hits me hard because of what it would mean about those I love who have already passed away.

A big part of my healing process when my mom died revolved around the idea that she wasn't really gone, that she lived on in some form or another, and even if I couldn't see her, I could feel her presence. I knew we would meet again—even if I wasn't completely sure when or what "meet again" could be. Same for Ana, and Brandon, and all the other amazing people I've loved and who have left this life. Seeing this loss as other than permanent separation helped get me through the loss. A lot of people grieve this way.

If they all were reduced to nothing, never to be seen by me again, well, that breaks my heart right down the middle. My mother and sister never knew me as an adult, a world-traveling musician, a yoga instructor, a husband, or a father. I like to think that they somehow are aware of the arc and details of my life today and are joyful about how it's all going. Could be just a coping mechanism, I suppose, but there's nothing wrong with coping.

It's not that I need their validation for my life to have been worthwhile. On the contrary, my life has been so rewarding and joyful that it really doesn't matter who else knows or appreciates it. But then, my life has been that way in part *because of* people who have since passed away. I owe them so much. To be able to see them again, to express my gratitude, and show them how far their love carried me would be amazing. The idea of not being able to do that is, naturally, sad.

Of course, the idea of nothingness can make our own death feel heavier. If I died tomorrow and knew that someday my wife and daughter would meet me again in heaven, well, I could presumably find great joy in waiting patiently while they lived their own fulfilling lives. If I died tomorrow and became *nothing* . . . well, *fuck*, I'd never see them again, and that's unbearably sad.

Though, if I was nothing, then I couldn't be sad. I could only be nothing.

The lighter side of eternal oblivion

But let's try to see another side to the story here. What if eternal nothingness isn't all bad? Yes, the whole "not seeing your loved ones ever again" thing is pretty freaking sad; but we're here to explore all of these death scenarios with open minds and hearts. Could endless nothingness have its upside?

Well, again, there would be no sadness in you if you

were reduced to nothingness. Maybe for the people you left behind, but you wouldn't miss being alive, not even for a second. Death would also mean the end of any sadness for your loved ones, too. So nothingness equals zero sadness. Technically, that's not *all* bad, right?

The suffering-versus-pain argument is irrelevant here. Both of them go away when you become nothing. If we consider the rebirth scenario, where we have perhaps endless cycles of birth, suffering, and death, getting it all over once and for all can seem at least a little bit appealing.

Our loved ones might find peace in nothingness as well. I watched my mother endure great pain through her cancer. When she passed away, I knew she was no longer in pain. If I had to make her go through that pain again, just to spend more time with her, I wouldn't be able to ask (though she would have done it in a heartbeat). Would we rather our loved ones be forever free from pain, or that we get to spend more time with them? Not an easy question— it asks us to be selfless and to hope for what's best for them, even if it's extremely painful for us. Yes, I would want to see my mom again. No, I would not want her to suffer anymore. In the nothingness scenario there is no middle ground. We cannot see our people again, but we can know that their suffering has ended forever. That seems positive to me, in its way.

Perhaps the most positive thing we could hope to get out of the eternal nothingness scenario is the freedom it might offer us in our day-to-day lives. If there is no heaven to strive for, no hell to avoid, then you're free from ultimate worries about the future. You can live more for this present moment. And if this life is to be your one and only life, you might be motivated to live well. That's two of our favorite things right there: living well, and the present moment!

Suffice to say that I don't mean "living well" in an endless-party, buy-and-consume-tons-of-cool-stuff way but in the following-your-dreams, being-kind-to-others, and making-a-difference way. The type of life after which, once you're gone like a fart in the wind, people left behind will remember you as far more than just that fart. And of course, what better time to create your legacy than the present moment?

So get to it! Your body may stop functioning, your consciousness may disappear forever, but as long as you lived well, someone will remember you fondly. Then a part of you lives on—and even if it doesn't, you'll have absolutely no idea, because you'll just be, peacefully, nothing.

12

Universal Oneness

An authentic life is a different sort of life. Unrehearsed behaviors lead to spontaneous interactions. A day spent with no expectations leads to unexpected wonders. A simple moment becomes an infinite moment, carrying with it the implications of total power.

—DON MIGUEL RUIZ

WHAT'S THE OPPOSITE of nothing?

Everything!

What if—instead of our being doomed to eternal oblivion—the truth of our lives and deaths ultimately is that we are, always have been, and always will be *the entire universe*? I for one have found a lot of peace through playing with this very big idea, which boils down to this: we are all part of one thing, we are experiencing it now, and when we die there's still the one thing. (Granted, it's not an idea that naturally makes a lot of sense to us at first. The oneness of the universe isn't easily grasped intellectually; it's maybe more a feeling than a thought. But let's give it a shot.)

If you've developed a steady meditation practice, perhaps you have at some point experienced a moment of actual silence, in which your mind is, even for just a split second, free from perceptions, thoughts, distractions. And in that moment of silence, maybe you've felt a deep sense of connection. (If you don't have a meditation practice, then you obviously will never have any idea what I'm talking about—*kidding!* I'm not a snob, at least not *that* much of one. This feeling of deep connection I'm talking about is actually quite common, and I think almost all of us will feel it at least once in our lifetime, if not many, many more times. Meditation or not.)

That feeling of connection is generally more available to us than we think. We often experience it and don't even realize that's what's happening! I talk a lot in *I Wanna Be Well* about mindfulness, whether it be walking, or eating, or listening to music. The basic idea is we let go of distractions and focus as fully as we can on doing one thing at a time. It's a very simple, yet profoundly powerful approach to life. I'll share a practice after this chapter to help you dip your toe into letting go of distractions, but for now, let's just think about this connection, times we may experience it, and what it might mean.

From Wyo to Peru

I grew up in the state of Wyoming—and the nature around there is truly awe-inspiring. Mirror Lake in the Snowy

Mountain Range, Medicine Bow National Forest, and the rock formations at Vedauwoo are all a short drive from my childhood home. I could tell you *all about* how amazing and beautiful these places are, but my words would fail in comparison to the actual experience. But even if you've never heard of or been to these places, you can probably still relate to something about them. When I take the time to be out anywhere in nature, away from the distractions of day-to-day life, I can find a deep, peaceful silence. In such moments I can be overcome by the feeling that things really are more connected than we think they are. It's quite possible you've tasted a similar feeling in the natural landscapes you've encountered. It isn't exclusive to Wyoming!

Through my travels I've experienced that feeling of connection all around the world. From the Izumo Taisha temple in Japan, to the ancient ruins of Machu Picchu in Peru, I've again and again been inspired by and overwhelmed with the sense that I am part of something endlessly greater than my individual self. Often it's been in nature, but if we're open to look for it, we might find it almost anywhere.

Think back. Can you recall moments in your life where time seemed to stand still, and everything was perfect, even if only fleetingly? Maybe it was simply losing yourself in your favorite song. Perhaps it was your wedding day, or the birth of a child. Maybe it was an epic sunset, a moment of stillness on a calm morning, or a bite of a *super*-good taco. Maybe you were fucking. It can be a big great moment, or it can be a beautifully simple moment, but if you've experienced any moment of real connection, there's no denying it. But just how deep does that connection go?

It can sometimes be easy to feel connected to our loved ones or to a moment, but what if that's just the tip of the iceberg? What if every single person, animal, plant, planet, star, and all of the space in between was all part of one thing? And even if that were true, what does this have to do with death? I'm glad you asked.

There are many ancient and modern views about what universal oneness might be like, but I think the philosopher Alan Watts might've nailed it by proposing that *we are the universe experiencing itself.* Let's go deeper with that.

Let's suppose that the universe is one thing.

And, for example, this one-thing of a universe would simultaneously be having the experience of being Miguel Chen, writing this book in 2018, and being you, reading this book at a later date. The universe would also be experiencing being my coauthor Rod wincing as he fixes my writing in 2018, while at the same time being some star deep on the other side of the galaxy—in 2018, in the future, and all the way back to the Big Bang, all at once.

Every speck of dust, every human being, all of the space in between—in this view we think of *all* that as the universe experiencing itself. If that's true, then life, death, and everything in between are perhaps just an experience that we (all of us here in the universe) are both creating and experiencing at the same time.

From this perspective, we see that we don't ever really die, at least not in the way we normally think of death. If we are the universe, we are timeless, without a beginning or an end. We just *are*, always. When my time experiencing what it's like to live as Miguel Chen in this time and place has come to an end, then my time to experience dying as Miguel Chen begins. And once that is over, whatever "I" was just takes some other new form, as some part of the universe. Sounds a lot nicer than fading into oblivion or burning in hell, at least.

This has some real significance as regards the loss of our loved ones, too. If I am the universe, then so was my sister, and my mother, and everyone I've ever loved who has passed away. And if they—*we all*—are the universe, then they—we—can never totally be gone, right? In one form or another, our loved ones are present as part of the universal whole. They are a part of us, we are a part of them, and not even death can change that.

The idea that we are the universe experiencing itself has a sort of healing power in daily life, too. As we noted before, it can be said that all of the world's problems come from separation. (I would say that myself.) People get attached to rigid ideas and concepts of self and don't like having those ideas threatened. Anger, hate, and greed all come from a feeling of separation, an *I want this so you can't have it; I need to protect myself* sort of thing. We hurt others, not recalling that they are part of us and we are part of them. We fail to see the interconnectedness of all things. A lot of people live as though the best way to advance their own lives is to fight against others, that there can't be enough resources or success for all of us, so it's every person for themselves.

Universal oneness kicks that idea to the curb. If we are all part of the same, abundant, infinite universe, we can begin to see that the separation we create is the cause of our suffering. If we hurt others, we hurt ourselves. If we help others, we help ourselves. If there is no limit to the universe, there is no limit to success, and by working together we can all be abundant and well. We can trash the *Us versus Them* mentality.

All there really is is *Us.*

13

PRACTICE:
A Lack of Distraction, a Moment of Wholeness

SINCE THE IDEA of universal oneness can be challenging, even if we understand it on an intellectual level, it's worthwhile to try and experience it for ourselves. This practice, which builds on your "Meditation Foundation" (page 21), can help. This will require a degree of consistency, so we'll start simply, by committing to a week of practice.

Plan ahead, and choose different locations for every day this week in which you will conduct this practice. It can be your bedroom, the library, an office, whatever. But have at least one day be out in some sort of natural setting. If you choose to have more than one day be outside, have it be in different places each time. Here we go.

On the first day

1. Once you've arrived at your location, turn off your phone and put away any other immediate distractions. There may be some distractions inherent with your location of choice (dogs barking outside, for example), but that's okay. We're not here to control everything, we're just here to experience.

2. Sit comfortably.

3. Notice your breathing for a few minutes, then as best you can, allow your mind to settle. From a mental perspective, that's it. We're not here to think or analyze our experience. With a relatively calm mind, just allow any sensations to come and go of their own accord.

4. Notice these sensations, but don't hold on to them. Allow them to drift away as easily as they came up in the first place.

5. After 10 minutes or longer, return to your breathing and end the session.

6. Write down any sensations that have stuck with you. Then put away your notes and go about your day. It's important to only think about the sensations that stay with you naturally. This will keep you from trying to hold on to anything during your practice.

Days 2 through 6

Repeat the process, but in a different location. Remember, at least one should be an outdoor, natural setting. Same as before, immediate distractions get put away, distractions inherent with the location are accepted as they are. Go through your breathing and calming practice, and write down any noteworthy sensations when you are finished.

Day 7

Find one last different location, and review your notes from the entire week. Sit and reflect on any similarities in your notes from day to day, as well as any differences.

Did you encounter stillness? A feeling of oneness? Nothing even remotely resembling that? Whatever you found, please share with the entire class over at my author Facebook page.

14

The Ones We
See Coming

Times like a health scare or a near accident are so simple and straightforward, so immediate. 'This is it,' we think. 'It's actually happening.' In such moments, the heightening of our awareness of death simultaneously heightens our feeling of being alive.

—JUDY LIEF

DEATH HAPPENS to us all—just not in the same way. Just as there are infinite variables that make up a person's life, there are infinite variables that can define their death.

It would be impossible to explore all of them, but we can begin by breaking things down into two categories: the deaths that we can expect or "see coming," and those that come, seemingly, out of nowhere. (Some might argue that, in a way, you can see *all* deaths coming. Maybe, but it could also be said that, really, one can never be prepared for any death. Neither is wrong. For our purposes, let's suppose some deaths are easier to see coming than others.)

Life expectancy may be higher than it's ever been, but we aren't made to run forever. Even the healthiest, luckiest, whatever-iest among us will have to die. Because of this, when someone dies of old age, we reassure ourselves that they'd had a good, long life. It seems less tragic than when someone dies relatively young, "before their time."

Think of your grandparents—whether you knew/know them or not. For a lot of folks, a grandparent's death from old age or natural causes might be their first experience of death. That was the case with my maternal grandfather, who died when I was too young for me to recall him. I couldn't understand the gravity of the situation. All I could comprehend, in my way, was that sometimes people were alive, and sometimes they weren't.

Now, my other three grandparents, I have wonderful, vivid memories about. I remember spending summers in Cuernavaca, Mexico, with Mama and Gaga, as we called my father's parents. I remember *Abuela* Emma coming to stay with us for a few months in Wyoming and the amazing breakfasts she would cook. I love these people deeply, and they loved me back.

My maternal grandmother is still with us today, and I am so grateful.

My father's parents both passed away within a few years of each other. I think about and miss them a lot, but they both lived what we could consider to be long, full lives, well into their golden years. This type of death would be in the "saw it coming" category; in the back of my mind I always knew they wouldn't always be there. Then one day they weren't. Even if it was sad, it seemed natural.

There are other instances when we can see death coming. Pets, for example. If you've ever gotten a puppy, somewhere in the back of your mind you are aware that the puppy will grow up into an adult dog, then an old dog, and someday it will pass away. But that's in the *back* of your mind, not the front of it! We don't want to dwell on this fact and become miserable. We want, instead, to maintain a gentle awareness that deepens our appreciation. If we've got a relatively long time to know death is coming, then we have a relatively long time to appreciate the time we are blessed with.

But just how long is "relatively long"? Relatively long doesn't always mean 78 years average age expectancy or 77 dog years. Relatively long is just that, relative.

And what about when illness itself is a long-term thing? My mother fought cancer for many years. During the last bout we knew her time was coming to an end. It wasn't an "old age" situation, but we did have some time to prepare for her passing. Once vibrant, energetic, and full of life, in the last year of her life she became still, quiet, and fragile. Her long brown hair was now short and gray; her glowing skin now a pale yellow. I didn't want her to leave this life.

But then one day she did. She was 51 years old. I was 16. Long-term illness like that is very difficult for everyone involved. And yet, strangely, it can bring with it a bit of a blessing: time. What we do with that time is up to us. In the case of my mother, I have regrets. I wish I could say that once I realized her time was coming to an end I became the perfect son and spent all of my extra time with her, taking in all her knowledge and love, making sure I would carry as much of her through the rest of my life as possible. I didn't. I spent a lot of that time in avoidance, trying to run from the inevitable truth. I would spend time with my friends, riding BMX, playing guitar, drinking, doing anything I could to avoid facing the truth.

Luckily, my mother, with the help of friends, insisted on having me by her side the last few days. I can't tell you how much of a blessing even that little bit of time was. We were able to share so much love and talk through any old problems we'd had. By the time she had died, I knew we'd built a completely uncompromised connection, full of love and free from unnecessary bullshit. This was the great gift of seeing that her death was coming. We had *time*.

Given a choice, would you want to know your own expiration date? How would you spend your time if you knew it would soon end?

In my mother's case, the first diagnosis of cancer was by no means seen as a death sentence. So she fought, as I believe most of us would. Eventually, she decided she didn't want to spend her life fighting. In a deeply self-compassionate decision, she decided to stop pursuing treatments she felt were only delaying the inevitable.

That changed everything. In a very real way, the moment my mother accepted that she was going to die, she became more alive than ever. Free from the crippling side effects of chemotherapy and experimental treatments, she was finally able to be truly present with the disease, and herself. She was able to let go of illusion, fully embracing both life and death, and spend the last few months of her life feeling, above all, deep love and connection.

What's the lesson? Maybe it all boils down to how we want to use our time. When you truly accept that time is finite, each moment becomes precious. If you have time (and we all do), try to use it. This doesn't mean obsessing over death and the fact that everyone we love will be gone. It means letting people know you appreciate them. Resolving old issues. Dropping unnecessary baggage. Do your best to know when to fight, and when to soften and let go. If you're reading this, if you're breathing, you have time. It's amazing how much life we can fit into just a little bit of time.

And if you've missed out on time, try not to beat yourself up. Just as we don't want to obsess over death, we don't want to obsess over things that we can't change. If you're sad that you've missed time with loved ones, forgive yourself.

Much better to spend your energies enjoying whatever time you *do* have. Which, of course, you can only guess. Which brings us to . . .

15

The Ones We Don't See Coming

I want to die like my father, peacefully in his sleep, not screaming and terrified, like his passengers. —BOB MONKHOUSE

DEATH IS AS unpredictable as it is inescapable: accidents happen, and accidental or unexpected deaths—the "ones we don't see coming"—happen. *Every* time we see a friend or loved one could be the last time. What do we do with that?

On that fateful Fourth of July many years back, I could have no real idea that my time with my sister was ending. I'd even say that, that day, for the first time in months, there was a feeling of lightness. Things had been dark, difficult, sad, and slow in the months since my mother had passed.

Adjusting to life without her was no easy task, and it had taken its toll on my father, my sister, and myself.

Still, time did what it does: it kept going. And with it came a (very) gradual healing. We weren't okay, far from it, but things had started to calm down to the point where at least we could see that life would, in fact, go on. My sister had big dreams, of going to study fashion, of continuing her involvement in multicultural groups to help promote and celebrate diversity. I had dreams of playing punk music and partying like an idiot. That Fourth of July, all our dreams seemed like they could still someday come true. It was a really beautiful day and time spent with my sister that I treasure deeply.

But on the fifth of July, I received a phone call that would haunt me for many years. A car accident had left my sister dead.

I was completely blindsided. My only sibling, my beloved sister Ana Suin, gone.

Just when we'd been starting to feel like things might someday be kind of okay, now this.

It would be the first completely *unexpected* death in my life, and certainly one of the most devastating. Over time, I would lose other friends unexpectedly, all deeply painful, but none as soul-crushing as the loss of Ana Suin. It felt like nothing could ever be okay again. Again.

I felt stuck, but time had its own plan. Time didn't care how much I hurt. It just kept going on, and so did I.

Brother Brandon

In the years after my sister's death, twin brothers Ray and Brandon Carlisle became like family to me. They took me under their wing and helped me focus in on music as a somewhat healthy means of dealing with life. Eventually I would join their band, Teenage Bottlerocket, and along with the other guitarist Kody Templeman, this new family model was complete.

Together we would live our dreams, making records, touring all over the world, and becoming friends with our favorite bands. From tiny dive bars in Wyoming to theaters in Japan and festivals in Europe, the four of us adventured together through the highest of highs and the lowest of lows. Brandon, Ray, Kody, and me; a family in the deepest sense.

The year 2015 would be an especially standout, successful year for the band, with a new record and shows all around the world, all capped off with an appearance at one of our favorite festivals: the annual Fest in Gainesville, Florida. After our set there, Brandon, his girlfriend, my girlfriend (now wife), Émilie, and I went out for some drinks to celebrate. I had planned on going straight to bed and taking it easy, but something told me I should instead go have fun with my brother Brandon. So I did, and we talked and talked and laughed and laughed. Best night ever. We felt so proud of everything we had accomplished together and couldn't wait to see what was next. We had absolutely no idea our time together was ending.

Brandon and the rest of the band flew home the next morning while I stayed in Florida to spend a couple extra days with Émilie. Tour was over, everyone would go their own ways, and then we'd see each other again soon for our next adventure.

I'd been home for two days before I got a phone call

from Ray: Brandon was in the hospital on life support. His roommate had found him unresponsive on the couch. I immediately drove to Fort Collins, Colorado, where Brandon had been living for a few years. The Intensive Care Unit was a heavy fucking place to be. We'd take turns going in to see Brandon, who was hooked up to all sorts of wires and monitors, only breathing thanks to a machine that was doing the work for him.

No one knew what to say or how to act. We all just waited, mostly in silence, for news.

Little by little, other friends and family of Brandon trickled in, all hoping to see Brandon come out of that coma and back into our lives. He would not.

Brandon's unexpected death was felt immediately, and deeply, by the worldwide punk rock community. Thousands of people came together, sending messages of love and support: from fans who had met him once, to some of the biggest bands in the world, all hoping Brandon would pull through and mourning deeply when he did not. Ray, Kody, and I had no idea what would be next for us. Our lives had been built around playing music and traveling with our best friend, our brother Brandon. Now he was gone.

Tragedy and perfection

These unexpected deaths, at least in my life, seem to come more often than those I could "see coming." Since Brandon has died, I've lost many other friends and family members to unexpected death, including one of my favorite aunts in a bus accident. You've probably lost loved ones in unexpected ways as well. So, you know: it is different when we don't see it coming. How? Why?

For starters, we're without the "luxury" of time when someone dies unexpectedly. Unlike when someone dies of old age or natural causes, we can't make a point of saying our good-byes, letting the person know how much we appreciate them. We can't work through old problems together or "wrap things up."

If someone dies unexpectedly and the two of you got into an argument the last time you saw them, it can weigh heavily on you. We're left with questions. Did they know how we felt? Did they know how much we loved them? The time to ask is gone, and we are left to wonder, uncertain and sad.

Another big difference when the death is sudden or unexpected might be the sense of *tragedy* we feel. Yes, it is sad when our grandparents, who we love, die. But at least we can comfort ourselves and say they had a long, happy life. When someone dies out of nowhere, we can't help but feel a sense of injustice: they didn't get enough time. The *world* didn't get enough time with *them*. They died too *young*. Their time was *cut short*.

An unexpected death certainly seems more tragic. So how do we deal with that?

For starters, we need to work with the idea that things are as they are and try to find some amount of acceptance. In my first book, *I Wanna Be Well*, I talk a lot about the perfection of the present moment. I realize it can seem pretty fucking hard to find anything *perfect* or *wise* in the present moment when we're talking about the unexpected death of a loved one. However, it's there.

We can sit around and wish as hard as we can for things to be different, we can try to hide ourselves from what's happening, but the truth will always be the truth. So we might as well learn how to soften ourselves and abide that truth. Letting go of how we wish things were is a key first step in the healing process. Things are as they are and always will be, and trying to accept that can be a great practice in self-compassion.

We can work in this way both with deaths that have already occurred and deaths that might someday occur. Knowing that death and life are both unpredictable, we can make it a point to appreciate each day, moment, and interaction on a deeper level. If we start each day with an awareness that it could be our last one, we will naturally gravitate toward the things that fill us with gratitude and joy. With this mind-set, we can let go of the things that don't really matter and make room, here and now, for the things that do. We can make it a point to let people know how much we love or appreciate them on a regular basis. We can work through any problems we might have with others now, because we can understand that our time with them is not guaranteed.

And, of course, no one can take away our memories, which can help us come to terms with our losses, and renew our love for people now gone, throughout the rest of our own lives. I'll always remember and love my sweet sister Ana Suin; her love of people and cultures, how she cared for and loved those around her. I'll always remember and love my best friend Brandon. I'll always feel blessed for the time we had to live out our dreams together.

Whether or not their deaths were more tragic than those I "saw coming," I can't say. What I can say is that what time we had together was invaluable, and death can't change that.

16

PRACTICE:
Prep Work

IF WE ACCEPT that death can be around any corner, then we can also accept that today is inherently valuable. This practice is about making time, today, to tie up some loose ends. We are, in a way, doing prep work for death; expecting but not obsessing over the unexpected.

This is a practice to be done at the beginning of the day. As with our other practices, it's best to start from a place of relative quiet and stillness. Grab a pen and paper, find your quiet place, and let's begin.

1. Sit comfortably.
2. Take a few moments to breathe deeply; allow your mind to settle down. You have nothing to do for now but breathe. Let any stray thoughts softly drift away as you come to a place of relative stillness.

3. Now, consider this (hopefully) imaginary scenario: Today is your last day on earth. Tomorrow, you will be gone. Sit with this thought for several moments. Breathe it in. Say it to yourself: *Today is my last day on earth. Tomorrow, I will be gone.* Notice any accompanying sensations that arise. *Today is my last day on earth. Tomorrow, I will be gone.*

4. Now, begin to consider: if that were true, what things would you need to do today? *Any* thoughts that come up are valid. *If tomorrow I'll be dead and gone, what do I need to do today?*

5. Grab your pen and paper. At the top of the page, write: *Today is my last day on earth. Tomorrow, I will be gone. Today I must:*

6. Now list a handful of the thoughts that have come up. Five to ten will suffice. If you were dying tomorrow, what would you want to do today? There are no wrong answers.

7. Once you have your list of five to ten items, I want you to read them one by one. Try to understand *why* each item made the list.

8. Now begin to look at the list objectively. Let's start from the really huge, grand ideas of what you would do with your day, and work down the list to the more subtle items on the list. For example, some might want to spend their last day on earth quitting their job and throwing a huge destination beach party with all of their friends and family. Some might just want to call an old friend and work through a fight from years ago. The list is yours; again, anything is valid.

9. Now, find the one item on your list that feels most manageable. You might not be able to go skydiving while juggling fireballs this afternoon (or maybe you might), but you can probably call that old friend you've been meaning to reach out to. Pick the one, most manageable thing on your last day on earth to-do list. Then do it. Your mind will try to resist, giving you seemingly solid reasons why you should not to do this one thing, or why you should just wait for another day. Don't. Remember, this could very well be your last day; you must do at least one thing on your last day to-do list. Even this one item will bring great freedom. If today really does end up being your last day, you can end on a high note.

17

By One's Own Hand

You know suicide isn't painless / when you leave everyone in pain. —"DOORNAILS" BY NOFX

SO WE'VE BEEN thinking about death in broad terms—the ones we "see coming" and the ones that are seemingly "out of nowhere." But we all know that death isn't easily defined in broad terms. Death is complicated, nuanced, difficult to categorize; it raises more questions than it answers.

One kind of death is perhaps the hardest to wrap our minds around: suicide.

I have, at the time of this writing, recently lost another friend to suicide. He had been dealing with deep depression for a very long time. I guess it finally became too much. His death was, as all suicides are, extremely tragic and left many of us mourning his loss.

Regarding this death, I felt like it came out of nowhere—and also that I could kind of see it coming. (In my experience, many suicides are like this.) We could all tell our friend was hurting for a long time, and we would make lots of effort to check in and help where we could. So, yeah: we could see this death coming in a way. Simultaneously, we weren't *truly* prepared for the possibility that our friend would take his own life.

I've noticed some common factors in most of the suicide deaths I've experienced. For starters, suicidally depressed people can be some of the most loving, caring individuals you could hope to meet. They feel deeply: love and joy, and also sadness and despair. Chronic depression can haunt them. I know firsthand, having spent many years dealing with my own depression and suicidal thinking.

I would never try to speak for every depressed or suicidal person. But I do have some things to say. First: depression, or suicidal thinking for that matter, doesn't make a person weak, or cowardly, or any of that bullshit some people say. We can't ever fully understand what it is to walk in another person's shoes. If we want to try, what's needed is our compassion, not our judgment. There is deeply ingrained pain in the heart of a suicidal person.

In my case, that pain came from losing my mother and my sister at a young age. I didn't know how to process that pain, and so I suffered daily. I would sit and literally wish that I had died instead of my sister or fantasize about alternate realities where I got to have what I thought to be a "normal" or "happy" life. Unable to accept what was true, I lived in a crippling internal hell. I just wanted the pain to be over, and in my mind, somehow dying would make that possible.

These days, I have a wife and child, and I love them more than anything. And I love what I do. I still can get deeply sad, though—as with my friend's recent suicide. Sometimes the sadness comes on for seemingly no reason at all. But I have tools that help: I meditate daily, I practice yoga, I write, and I play music. When something hurts, I take the time to investigate it and to feel what I need to feel. I no longer want to die (or at least I wanna die *way* less often). I know I am fortunate to have made it out the other side of chronic depression and suicidal thoughts. Not everyone is. Luckily, there are many resources available to us: access to support groups, counselors, and therapists is available online and IRL, and practices such as meditation are available for anyone to learn.

So, how do we work with death by suicide?

For starters, we must do everything we can do to prevent it. There are common warning signs we can recognize. A person contemplating suicide might:

- frequently withdraw from social activities. They begin to create a distance between themselves and others, which can make their depression and suicidal thoughts even more formidable.
- begin to make preparations. I've had friends who came back to town to have a drink with all of their old acquaintances, and only after their death did we realize they were saying good-bye.

- give away prized personal possessions or purchase instruments for the death itself, such as a gun or drugs. Sometimes, too, a suicidal person will joke or laugh about killing themselves. (Of course, sometimes a joke is just a joke, but sometimes it's more, and as friends we need to try to tune in to the nuances.)

If you think a friend is hurting, reach out. Call, text, stop by—engage with them as best you can. You might not be able to take their pain away, but you can listen and show that you care. A suicidal person needs to know they're not alone.

And while we don't want to intrude upon anyone's privacy, if you suspect self-harm is imminent, you may well want to reach out to loved ones or authorities.

Sometimes, however, nothing we can say or do will help. We can try all we want, but a person who is intent on committing suicide might still find a way. I know that's harsh, sad, and unbearable, but that's part of it.

What to do when a suicide has already happened

First, forget about blaming yourself. We can kick ourselves for not seeing the signs and not doing enough to prevent a suicide, but again: some deaths we'll see coming, and some we won't.

The victim doesn't deserve blame, either. And blame won't make a positive difference. So, as best you can, let it go. This is a deeply compassionate gift we can give to ourselves and everyone else who's survived this kind of loss.

And, as with any death, we need to find some level of acceptance so that we may move forward in life. This always takes time, and the sense of not knowing and tragedy that comes with suicide complicates things: it feels as if someone is gone "before their time," or as if a different set of circumstances could have prevented this loss. Let yourself feel what you need to feel—but try not to get stuck in those feelings. Step by step, piece by piece, work through it at your own pace. Remember those resources available to you: from meditation to medication to grief counselors, support groups, friends, and family. Using these resources, you'll know you're not alone in your pain and that it won't be unmanageable forever.

And don't exhaust yourself trying to "make sense" of suicide. There's no making sense of it. Try and accept that it's not your job to *understand*, but rather to *accept* and to heal. Being of service to others can help immensely, so make yourself available to others who are hurting if you can. But also give yourself time to hurt as well.

And what if it's you who is deeply depressed or suicidal?

"You're not alone." "It gets better." Yes, these are clichés, but they're not bullshit—you're *not* alone, and things *do* get better. When we're attracted to the certain sense of power and control that taking our own life seems to offer us, we need to be reminded just how much power and control there is in making our lives ones that we want to keep. (Besides, what makes us so sure that dying will cause our pain to stop? We have no idea what happens after death, so let's work with what we do know: life.)

If you need help, reach out to someone. If you don't know who to reach out to, call the National Suicide

Prevention Hotline. 1-800-273-8255. They will, for sure, hear you. And remember: just as there's no shame in talking, there's no shame in taking psychiatric medication if you need it.

Assisted suicide

There's one case where perhaps taking one's own life isn't quite as tragic and sad. If a person is in chronic pain, counting down the days of a terminal diagnosis, should they be able to decide when to end their life?

Medical aid in dying, at the time of this writing, is legal in some countries and in seven of the United States. It's a complicated, emotional issue for sure. Since I have never been terminally ill (*duh*), I only know secondhand how incredibly painful a terminal disease can be. Though I watched my mother pass away from cancer, I can't begin to imagine what that's like firsthand.

You can have your own thoughts and feelings about assisted suicide. I'm not here to try and sway you in one direction or the other. But I do think there's a good way to think about all this: *when someone else is making decisions about their life, it's best to try and see it from their point of view.*

Personally, I believe that if a chronically ill person wants to end their life, that should be their right; they should be offered medical and emotional support, and their wish should be granted. Many state and country laws, however, maintain a different view. As for the rest of us—friends, family, loved ones—it's important to remember that this is not about *us*. The most compassionate thing we can do is support our loved one. It won't be easy, but again: support groups, meditation, and other resources can help.

In all likelihood, you or someone you know will be affected by suicide, assisted or not. It won't be easy. It's in our nature to try and make sense of life and death, and suicide challenges that part of us. Perhaps the hardest thing to accept is that we can never fully understand and that that's okay. If we soften our need to understand, we will have removed a major obstacle on our path to healing. The mind doesn't need to *understand* pain for the heart to process it.

18

By Another's Hand

A man's dying is more the survivors' affair than his own.

—THOMAS MANN

IF YOU THOUGHT that last chapter was heavy, you may really want to hold on to your butt for this one . . .

What happens when death is brought upon us by someone else?

Death at the hand of another can seem particularly senseless. These deaths can also be complicated and difficult to categorize. There are many ways to kill, or be killed by, another. Some are intentional to varying degrees, some are completely accidental, and many lie somewhere in the gray area in between. For our purposes, I want to consider three main subgroups of death by another's hand: accidents, murder, and war.

Intention, or lack thereof, matters here. There *is* a difference between deciding to murder someone and accidentally running them over—but even this isn't necessarily black and white. To try and make sense of it all, let's start simple, by considering accidental deaths where there was absolutely no intention involved.

Unintended killing

I never got to meet the guy who crashed his car into my sister's. In fact, I know absolutely nothing about him, except that he survived the crash with virtually no physical injuries. I do think it's safe to say that he did not intend to kill my sister that day. That didn't stop me from feeling tremendous anger toward him. If he hadn't been driving where he was, when he was, how he was, I'd likely still have a living sister.

For a long time, I tortured myself trying to understand how and why this could happen: *Was he paying enough attention? Did he do what he could to avoid the accident?* This need to understand what I might never be able to understand only put more suffering on top of the actual loss of Ana.

Luckily, I found a way to sit with, and through, the pain, after a series of fortunate events led me to a daily meditation practice. I'm not saying that's the answer for everyone. There are many ways to be present with *what is*, from walking through nature to playing a guitar, even something as seemingly simple as mowing the lawn or washing the dishes. But meditation was the door that led *me* to see the undeniable truth.

The truth was that my sister's death was an accident; completely tragic and soul-crushing, but an accident nonetheless. Coming to terms with this truth didn't make me any less sad, but it made me less angry, and that was a start. It always is. When anger clears, it makes room for compassion, which can be a powerful, healing force. Just as you can't be happy if you're busy being sad, you can't feel compassion if you're busy being angry. When I began to look at my sister's death through the lens of compassion, I realized I had been so wrapped up in the pain my family and I had gone through that I had never for a moment considered the other driver.

It can't be easy to know that someone has been taken from their loved ones and that that's happened, at least in part, because of you. As much pain as I was feeling, I had to acknowledge that the other driver had to be in some kind of pain now as well. This wasn't about comparing his experience to mine; how can such pain be quantified? It was about realizing that, in an accident, there are no winners and blame doesn't help. This same realization would help me tremendously when my aunt was killed in a bus accident years later. I saved a lot of time in the healing process by being able to let go of blame and, subsequently, anger.

Allowing ourselves to feel sad without pushing our sadness away can be incredibly healing. But we need to be careful not to get stuck. When the time comes to feel joy again—*and we will*—we must allow ourselves to feel that as well. Any accidental death, of course, will be incredibly sad for those of us left behind, but we can find some kind of peace knowing it was an accident, and there is no one to blame.

But what do we do when that's not the case? When there is clearly someone at fault in a death?

Senseless

I grew up in a town that would become famous for a horrible murder, one that would bring not just our state but the whole nation together to mourn and to create federal hate-crime legislation. The 1998 Matthew Shepard case still looms large for many people all these years later. (Twenty years later, in 2018, some sense of peace would be found as Matthew's remains were interred in the National Cathedral in Washington, D.C.)

Shepard was a young gay man and a student at the University of Wyoming. He was abducted, beaten senselessly, and left to die, tied to a fence outside of Laramie. He died in a hospital a few days later.

It was the first time I realized murder can happen anywhere, even in small-town Laramie, Wyoming. Murder isn't super-common in this town, though it does occasionally happen. I can't help but think of other areas of the world where murder is an almost daily occurrence, a harsh and constant reality of life. If you turn on the news, it's hard not to see stories about murder and mass shootings. It's senseless, and if we try to apply the "intent" lens to it, that doesn't help at all. It remains senseless and heartbreaking.

And those affected have a lot more they might feel: anger, rage, sadness, desperation, confusion, lack of safety, fear, doubt, disorientation—the whole gamut of emotions associated with loss. No one *wants* to feeling any of those things, but the reality is that *we have to* sometimes, and the loss of a loved one, especially if by way of an intentional act, is definitely one of those times.

But we can take our time. We can ask for help. And we can allow ourselves to feel what we need to feel, when we need to feel it. That includes the feeling of letting go.

DABDA

In response to any death we feel intimately, it helps to recall the famous 5 Stages of Grief, as put forth by Elizabeth Kübler Ross and David Kessler, and known by their initials, DABDA:

- Denial
- Anger
- Bargaining
- Depression
- Acceptance

We don't all process grief and loss in this exact way, but the DABDA framework (which we'll talk about in detail later) gives us a sense of what we might expect. At the very least we can know that processing after a death takes time, and that we might be in for a bit of a roller coaster ride.

We can work with that.

Once we've felt, say, the anger we need to feel, we can soften, even just a little, allowing ourselves to feel whatever comes next. Maybe it's the bargaining, "if only" stage; maybe it's sadness or depression. Whatever it is, *our* work is to let it come in and do *its* work—without clinging or identifying too much with it—and then to soften again, even just a little. And to be forgiving. Some will tell you that forgiveness is essential to healing; it certainly can't impede the process. No one expects us to forgive the unforgivable, but if we want to truly be free, we must let go.

This process can take time, and that's okay. As long as we take even just a tiny step toward letting go, we have done something compassionate and productive. There's real power in making that decision to heal. We can even make it through the unthinkable—even the loss of a loved one by an intentional act of murder. And if the lines of intention are blurry? We can work through that too.

Death during wartime

Let's touch on one last type of death at the hand of another, one as old as time and as relevant as ever.

I don't care to speculate here why war happens, if it will ever end, if it's necessary, or if we can end it and find world peace. I'd like to think that we *will* all know great peace someday, and I'm certain that every step we take to develop *inner* peace can only move us closer toward that. And surely, part of finding that type of peace has to do with processing the deaths of others. So what about those who die during war?

Intention becomes a particularly confusing aspect of such deaths for, in war, many are willing participants to some degree. Some soldiers are fighting because of a deep sense of duty, out of love of country, and to protect what they believe is an honorable way of life. Others are fighting to try and improve their lives or escape unthinkable situations. Some may become soldiers out of some version of what we might call socioeconomic necessity. Others may have been conscripted into fighting against their wishes. The one thing we can say for sure is that everyone who goes to war knows, at least a little, that they might not return.

These are people, very often young adults, with hopes and dreams about the lives they will build when they return from conflict. So it's unfathomably sad to see their dreams go unfulfilled, their lives not lived. We find some comfort, sometimes, in saying they died for their country, their beliefs. Death in the line of duty is honored, the sacrifice commemorated—but that doesn't make it easier. Even death that seemingly has some sort of purpose can feel completely senseless and unnecessary. All of the possible emotions may well present themselves here as well, and we will have to work through them.

Just as there are a zillion ways to die, there are a zillion ways to process. There's no formula, no "do A, B, and C if you lose a loved one to an accident," no to-do list for survivors to run through after a murder. One thing is true in every case: healing involves a lot of compassion, letting go, and acceptance. We can't change what has happened, but perhaps investigating what happens next can help, if even just a little.

Let's go!

19

PRACTICE:
Forgiveness Meditation

UNDERSTAND THAT holding on, especially to anger, can impede our ability to heal. You've likely heard the saying about holding on to anger being like drinking poison and expecting the other person to die. If someone you know has been killed, there most definitely will be anger involved. Even if you haven't lost anyone, chances are that anger has held you hostage at some point in your life. Maybe it still does. Our practice is to let go of that anger, so that we can heal and move forward. One way to do that is to cultivate our capacity to forgive.

So find your best quiet, distraction-free place and take a comfortable seat. After spending a couple of minutes simply breathing in and out, allow yourself to settle into this practice.

- First, consider a person you are angry at for some reason or another. (It is best to ease into this practice, so start with someone manageable. Someone who cut in line at the grocery store is easier to work with than someone who killed your sister in a car accident. We will practice with the more difficult people in our lives soon enough, but to establish our practice, it's good to take baby steps. So bring this person who has made you angry, but not traumatically so, to mind.)

- Spend several moments holding this person in your mind's eye. Allow any sensations, especially anger, to arise. We're not looking to suppress anything here. If anger shows its face, allow it, breathing it in and out completely.

- For some time, think about the way(s) this person has made you angry.

- Then start to settle back into stillness, consciously allowing things to soften, even just a little bit: unclench your jaw if it's clenched, let your shoulders drop if they've crept up, and breathe naturally.

- Begin to entertain the possibility that your anger is poison, and therefore, releasing it can help you heal. Notice any sensations (discomfort, resistance, or anything else) that arise as you consider this. It's okay; allow them to be present.

- Continue to maintain awareness of your breath and soften as best you can. Can you be open to the possibility of letting go of your anger? Even a little?

- Now, bring the person back to your mind's eye—only imagining them now as a child. A being who has not yet hurt anyone. A child not so different from how you were, with aspects of liveliness, love, and hope.

- Now offer the child forgiveness. Say to them, internally, *I forgive you. For all of the pain and anger you have caused, I forgive you.* Keep breathing, keep noticing anything that arises. Any resistance or anxiety are just as welcome as acceptance or peace. *I forgive you. For all of the pain and anger you have caused, I forgive you.* You don't need to mean it. Not at first. You simply have to try your best and repeat, *I forgive you. For all of the pain and anger you have caused, I forgive you.*

- Continue to breathe, soften, and offer, as best you can, forgiveness to this younger version of the person who has caused you pain. *I forgive you.*

- After several moments, begin to release the image from your mind. Let all words fade away, and sit in silence. Notice any remaining physical sensations. How does it feel, physically, to offer forgiveness? There are no right or wrong answers.

- Gently conclude your practice and move into the rest of your day.

This practice can take several attempts to make a difference, and that's okay. Keep at it. Start with manageable people; over time you can begin to confidently consider even those who have hurt you the most. Even if at first it feels insincere, "fake it till you make it." Keep on faking it as long as you have to. You have taken the first step, and that's huge.

20

Remains

Si vivimos como respiramos,
aspirando y dejando ir,
no nos quedemos equivocar.

—engraved on my mother's gravestone

THOSE HAVE BEEN my go-to words since we buried my mother's ashes in her birth town of Los Mochis. Their meaning: *If we live like we breathe, taking in and letting go, we can't go wrong.*

Whenever times are tough, I try to remember this final lesson from my mother. We *can* take life in fully, and we *can* also let go completely.

Letting go can be a protracted and painful process, especially when it comes to death. One major, usually early, milestone in the process is the physical act of dealing with the body of the deceased. It's tangible, definitive.

Cremation

In my family, we tend to be cremators. At least that's what we did with my sister, my mother, and our family pets. I'm not sure exactly *why* that's how we handle the bodies of our beloved family members, but it's what I've known. Maybe part of it is that since we buried my sister and mother in a family plot in Mexico, cremation just made more logistic sense. Flying to Mexico with a box of ashes is definitely less complicated than flying down with a full casket (although there most certainly were complications with the ashes as well).

From just an environmental perspective, it could be argued that dead bodies take up a lot of space, and cremation fixes the space issue, while also creating less waste. If you choose to bury ashes, you will need significantly less land to do so than for a casket. Or you can choose to scatter the ashes in nature, keep them in a box on your mantle, or even press them into a vinyl record, which can then live comfortably among your Ramones collection. (I haven't done that, but I totally would.) Cremation is also relatively low-cost, at least compared to burial.

But, modern concerns and logistics aside, why would we burn the remains of our deceased?

For as long as humans have been dying and other humans have been left to deal with their remains, cremation was adopted as a solution early on. We have reason to believe that our ancestors in the Stone Age likely employed cremation as a solution. Vikings would burn their dead because it was believed the smoke would carry the spirit to the afterlife. To this day in India, certain Hindu groups will burn their dead in elaborate rituals before sending them home down the Ganges River.

Part of all this—not to be *super*-obvious—is that there's something really powerful about fire. It doesn't only destroy; it cleanses. Think of land where a forest fire once ravaged all the tall trees, but in so doing gave room for saplings to sprout where they wouldn't have been able to before. Similarly, when a crematory fire or funeral pyre burns a lifeless body, we have no choice but to start letting go of our attachment to our loved one's physical form. Seeing the remains of our loved ones reduced to ash can be seen as the shedding of a vessel; they are free to move on. It can remind us that our loved ones were *never* only their bodies to begin with.

Burial

Many things about a casket/full-body burial make sense. For starters, the act of burning a loved one's body, even if they're done using it, might seem too intense or even disrespectful. I remember the last time I saw my mother alive, versus seeing her dead body, versus seeing her as a box of ash. All *very* different feelings. Some can find the idea of seeing their most beloved family members reduced to the contents of a tiny box unfathomable, and I don't blame them.

But, just as burning a body can be a practice in letting go, burying a body can similarly help us. We see, in a very immediate way, that our loved one is no longer inhabiting that body. Blood no longer flows through their veins, air no longer flows through their lungs. There's even a change in skin tone that quickly starts up when a person has passed away. I remember the immediate graying of my mother's skin seconds after she'd taken her last breath. There was no doubt about it: she was really leaving us.

Physically seeing the body also allows us a last chance to say good-bye "in the flesh." This can be good, but also not: in my sister's case, I never saw her body; the coroners suggested we remember her as she was, rather than as the accident had left her. I'm thankful for their wisdom. Seeing Brandon one last time in his casket was similarly powerful. I could tell for myself that he was no longer in that body, and it was time to say good-bye. (Though, I also had a deep feeling that he wasn't *really* gone, a feeling I still carry with me today.)

Burial, cremation: different approach, same result. Someone has died, and there is a transition inherent in that truth, waiting to be undergone whether you're burying your loved one, spreading their ashes, mummifying their corpse, or having them taxidermied onto their skateboard. (Probably not legal. Check local laws.) That transition has to be undergone even if there is no body to be dealt with, as in the case of a missing person.

I want my loved ones to decide for themselves what to do with my body. I'm partial to cremation, because that is what I have known, but what happens with a body—unless its previous owner had strong religious or other convictions to consider—is really for those who remain. I could be cremated and put in a box or shot off on a shuttle into space for all I care. What difference could it make to me? The healing process of those who loved me is all that would matter. I say "process," of course, because it's ongoing. It doesn't magically end the moment we bury or cremate a body. Connecting, remembering, honoring, and letting go are all ongoing work. How we do that work can have a profound impact on the rest of our lives.

Wait, did you say "tequila"?

In my native country of Mexico, many celebrate *Dia de Muertos* (Day of the Dead) at the end of October/beginning of November. (This just so happens to nestle right up to my sister's birthday.) There are rituals involving shrines, pictures, candles, and offerings such as sugar skulls or tequila. The idea is that our loved ones exist in a state beyond life, and that by honoring and remembering them, we keep their spirits alive. While I don't go the full ceremonial route, I do find it nice to spend some time reflecting on my family and connecting to their memory.

I have friends in Japan who have big elaborate shrines for their deceased as centerpieces of their homes, and it's awesome. Likewise, I try to keep pictures and special objects that remind me of my loved ones in key places where I live, sleep, and work. I've also known others who very intentionally *don't* keep pictures of their deceased around. That's fine too. What I'm getting at is that this process is different from person to person, from culture to culture, and from subculture to subculture. We each need to find what works best for us. If it helps you to connect, bury your loved ones nearby; if it helps to let go, spread their ashes somewhere special. You can write a song or a book, build a monument, start a memorial fund; you can do anything. Or nothing. Whatever you do or don't do, just remember: take in and let go, and you can't go wrong.

21

Life Goes On

Life is here, death is over there. I am here, not over there.
—HARUKI MURAKAMI, in *Norwegian Wood*

EXPLORING THE POSSIBILITIES of our existence (or nonexistence!) after death can be a healing process. It can sometimes even be kind of fun. And that's all good. But of course, it's mostly theoretical. We don't—and can't—be sure of what happens to us when we die. That information isn't ours to know, not yet at least.

One thing we *can* know: no matter what happens to someone after *they* die, those who are left behind will feel a huge impact. That's the realest of real-world stuff.

When someone we love dies before we do

As I was beginning work on this chapter, I received news of

yet another old friend dying; it happened a couple days ago, and I'm deeply sad.

But I must admit that I'm, somehow, collected and calm too. I've known a *lot* of people who have died. It's not that I'm desensitized, though. Instead, it's occurred to me with the passing of all these years, and people, that the reason I have so many friends who have died is because I have been blessed—blessed to have so many friends to begin with. Would I go back in time and prevent all their deaths if I could? Yeah, but that's not real. And so I'm left to deal with what *is*.

When someone we know dies, well, things change. The more we love someone, the bigger a part of our lives they were, the deeper the change we'll feel when they die. If a neighbor you wave to once in a while dies, you won't have them to wave to anymore. You might feel a little sad, but other than that the change is pretty minimal. If the dude with the taco stand passes away, you can't buy his tacos anymore, but there are more tacos out there, and your life can shift accordingly.

But if your father, mother, sister, brother, best friend, mentor, spouse, or child dies, that's a whole 'nother story:

- You can't call them on the phone
- You can't go out to lunch with them
- You can't ask them for advice on big life decisions
- You can't ask them for advice on raising your child
- You can't give each other support when you're feeling down
- You can't give them a big hug
- You can't cry on their shoulder

- You can't go to new or favorite places together
- You can't share new accomplishments with them
- You can't see them and tell them you love them
- and on and on and on.

How do we adapt to these changes? How do we process the pain of losing someone we love?

As with All Things Death (the name of my new goth boutique, by the way), there's no cookie-cutter answer. And yet, like clockwork, we all pretty much start off with avoidance and denial: alcohol or drugs; focusing on meaningful, or meaningless, distractions; degrees of nonacceptance. Those sorts of thing. It's not that these approaches can't work at all, but they're temporary fixes at best and can have long-term consequences.

You'll recall the Kübler-Ross model, or DADBA, introduced in Chapter 18. Let's dive in deeper. Formulated in 1969 to understand the process a terminally ill patient begins upon diagnosis, it has since been applied to processing the loss of another person as well. To review: the idea is that a person can expect to experience five states or stages when grieving a notable loss. They are:

- Denial
- Anger
- Bargaining
- Depression
- Acceptance

In recent years the DABDA model has come under scrutiny from those who contend that grieving can't necessarily be contained as a neat, five-step process. The model did originally present these five stages in a specific order, and it's important to note that, again, things don't always go that way. Some may never go through all five stages. Some, whether they do or not, may jump all over the place from one "stage" to another. But DABDA is a good solid framework for understanding what our internal grieving process *might* look like.

First up: **Denial**. Think about any movie ever where someone dies, and the other person yells out a dramatic *NOOOOOOOOOOO!* That's not just drama; it's DNA. When something happens that we don't want to happen, we want right away to fight it, and denial is our way of trying to fight off something that seems too terrible to be true. And not just about death, of course. Most of us spend portions of our lives in *some* sort of denial about who we really are and what we are really doing with our time. It's hard to look at ourselves honestly, and it's really fucking hard to be honest when we're reckoning with a death. Denial is our mind's last-ditch effort to try and act like everything is all right—when things are really, really, really not all right.

On July 5, 2002, when I got the call saying that something had happened to my sister, denial kicked in immediately. The caller couldn't tell me if my sister was alive or dead, she said; she needed to tell me in person. It would take only a few minutes for her to arrive at my house, but that was long enough to enter into a full-on state of denial. No way was my sister dead. It couldn't be her she was talking about. It couldn't be as serious as it sounded over the phone. Even when I'd heard the actual words that my sister was gone, I couldn't believe it. But denial or not, the truth was the truth.

Now, denial isn't *all* bad. (Just *mostly*!) It can ease the transition from our comfort zone into our new truth. It would have been pretty fucking weird if I'd been told my sister was dead, and my immediate reaction was an indifferent "Okay then, *that* happened." Denial happens because we're anything *but* indifferent. We're fighting, albeit misguidedly, for things to be the way we think they should be. We don't want to let go of our loved ones, and when we have to, denial is like a first step as we enter a new phase of life. Mine, as of that day, was that I would be without my sister from there on.

Denial is where many of us get stuck. Whether or not we do it consciously, the pain of losing a loved one can be so heavy that we go into long-term denial and avoidance. I know for sure I tried to do that for years. It wasn't until I could accept the truth that my healing could actually begin. So my advice? After the initial wave of denial passes, let it go. Denying the truth isn't helping any of us, even if the truth hurts like fucking crazy.

If we can't deny the truth, then, what *can* we do?

Well, we could resort to **Anger**, and a lot of us do. This, the second step in the Kübler-Ross model, is when we get angry about our loss. I think the intensity of this step, and whether or not we ever experience it, has a lot to do with individual personalities. Some people have a tendency to get mad more easily and for longer periods than others. In the case of my sister's death, my anger period was relatively short. I was mad for a bit at the other driver. I was mad for a while at God. Then I gave up. I couldn't be mad at a guy who didn't mean to kill my sister, and I couldn't be mad at a God I didn't really believe in. Still, with or without reason, anger is natural, especially when it comes to losing someone we love. But that anger isn't getting us anywhere. We can rage at the world, but we'll suffer for that in the end. So as best we can, we need to let anger go.

This brings us to **Bargaining**. When we lose someone we love, we can get desperate to have them back. People who have never had a religious thought in their lives can find themselves begging God for a different outcome. When it came to my sister, I prayed and prayed and made deals that could never be met. By the time we're driven to desperate bargaining, it's often too late. (Someone facing cancer might try to bargain, saying they will never smoke again, and that may be true, but the damage has been done.) The good news is we don't have to bargain for anything in order to be better versions of ourselves. In fact, the more we try to be our best and help those around us, the better we can heal our own pain.

Next on the Kübler-Ross model: **Depression**. Some may bypass denial, anger, and/or bargaining, but the loss of a loved one is very likely to start a period of some amount of depression. The very idea of losing someone forever *is* depressing.

As with denial, anger, and bargaining, depression is a natural reaction: again, we wish for things to be different, and when they aren't, we feel sad. Sadness isn't automatically bad, but we have to be careful not to get stuck there, because depression can haunt us for weeks, years, even entire lifetimes. And we *can* be sad without being chronically depressed. I still get sad about my mother's death, and it's almost 20 years later. I probably always will. But I also find joy in my daily life. I don't live in a constant sadness of loss, and you don't have to either.

The final step on the Kübler-Ross model is where our capacity for healing really begins to make itself felt: **Acceptance**. Now, we've explored in other chapters how pain and suffering differ. (To recap: we all must feel pain, but suffering is optional.) When someone we love dies, we can't ever hold them, or call them, or see them again. That's all painful, but we don't have to keep suffering. We can feel the pain we need to feel and then little by little make room for other feelings, including even joy again. That starts with acceptance.

Once I could finally accept that my mother and sister weren't coming back, I felt a huge fundamental shift in my attitude toward life. It was a long, drawn-out process, but at some point, I was happy again. Any of us can get there, but that depends on our acceptance of the truth.

That truth comprises two facts so obvious you'd think they never even have to be said, and yet we have to keep reminding ourselves: (1) Everyone dies, even the people we love. (2) Until it's our turn, life goes on. And as long as *you* have another day, another minute, another breath, there's the chance to reconnect with what's beautiful, with what matters.

When it feels like nothing can ever be okay again, remember: suffering can die, too.

22

Time to Die

If you are compelled by the idea that there is a way to awaken to something beyond birth and death, consider reflecting upon death. —LAMA SHENPEN HOOKHAM

SINCE DEATH CAN come at any time, in any form, we might as well be prepared. So, in a bit, we'll learn a practice that can help us do just that.

For now, let's think in terms of two types of death: not as we did before, with the ones we see coming and the ones we don't, but the ones that happen to others and the one that will happen to us. We should contemplate and work with both if we want to live to our fullest potential, or at least not get stuck in despair when death shows up.

Dealing with the deaths of others can sometimes be easier than dealing with our own death. This is because we aren't really given a choice. Whether or not we want to accept it, when someone we love dies, *boom*: we will have started the journey of dealing with the deaths of others. Our own death, though? We could theoretically live our whole lives without thinking about it until the very last second. Lots of us do.

I don't need to tell you that just because a buttload of people do something, that doesn't make it a good idea. And, as we've seen again and again, pretending something won't happen is hardly a wise strategy. But there's good news. When we're willing to think about death *at all,* that's us already heading in the right direction. From there we can investigate and maybe even come to terms with our own mortality. Connecting with the inevitability of "the death of you" can give you a deeper appreciation for the time that you *do* have. Death: It Enhances Life! (™)

Of course, it's easier to just wake up every morning, fall into our routines, and not take the time to think about our lives, much less our deaths. It's easier *not* to look unflinchingly at ourselves and admit that perhaps we have wasted a *lot* of our time. But if we want to stop wasting more of that time and start living in a more mindful way, thinking about our death can help.

But not too much. *Just* enough. Connecting to death in a beneficial manner is a practice. You want to walk the line between avoidance and obsession. That takes practice, and that's why we'll be going through a practice together.

But first: I know thinking about death can be scary. So diving into a deep meditation practice about it may be scary, too. That's probably okay. You can let yourself be scared. Just try to remember why you are doing this to begin with. The benefit—being freer from one of the most deep-seated fears we humans have—is great. It's like those cliché ideas about facing your fears—skydiving if you're afraid of heights, going to a circus if you're afraid of clowns. Facing down one of our fears can bring with it a tremendous feeling of aliveness. Especially this one.

Who gets my stuff?

Part of facing our fear of death can include the practical aspects of estate planning. There are legalities involved with dying and making sure your final wishes are carried out. None of us want to talk or think about this stuff, but it's important.

The first step is admitting to yourself that someday you will, in fact, be dead. Some of your loved ones will likely be around after you are dead. Thinking about that stuff can be scary, that's valid; however, NOT thinking about that stuff doesn't make it any less true and might leave those you leave behind twisting in the wind. Estate planning is about taking care of them. You can't control if/when/how/why you die; but you can reduce at least the financial impact your family will feel when it happens.

Life insurance, wills, trusts; they're all set up to help cover your final expenses, as well as designate where and how you want your assets located when your time comes. I'm not an expert on any of this, but an estate lawyer can help point you in the right direction. Furthermore, if you have children, estate planning lets you designate who would take care of them in the event both parents died suddenly. Again, not stuff any of us wanna think about, but something we definitely should think about. I'm a dad now and, as I said, I'm no expert, so I'm doing it. I've found it's all about getting past that initial fear and procrastination. Once you do, you will be rewarded with at least some peace of mind, knowing that even if you aren't around, your family will be taken care of.

Estate planning can be a practical way of tangling with the reality of our mortality and facing our fears on a material level. The practice that follows is a way to face those things on an existential or spiritual one.

23

PRACTICE:
Death Meditation

THE FRAMEWORK for the first half of this meditation can be attributed to Atisha, a Buddhist teacher from around a thousand years ago, who coined what became known as the nine contemplations of death. The second chunk of the practice is a more traditional death meditation, where we try to connect to the process of leaving our body. This part of the practice is based on a Theravada Buddhist practice known as *maranasati*, or mindfulness of death. As with other practices in this book, I've modified things so as to be nondenominational and accessible to anyone regardless of their beliefs.

Let's get started. As with any of our meditations, we gotta find a quiet place, relatively free from distractions. It's hard to focus on dying if your puppy is trying to lick your face or your best friend is texting you. Put the distractions away and set up your space.

We don't usually associate dying with being upright, so for this practice, let's lie down. To help make you sustainably comfortable, you may want to get a bolster or rolled-up blanket and slide it under your knees, and also find a small pillow or blanket to place under your head for support. You want to be comfortable but not so much so that you fall asleep. So commit now at the beginning of practice: *I will not sleep. I'm here to practice dying, not sleeping. I will NOT fall asleep.*

Once you're comfortably lying down, committed and in your distraction-free location, you can start our first contemplation:

1. Soften your gaze, breathe deeply, and relax into your posture. Inhale. Exhale. Let your mind settle, as best you can, for several moments.
2. Taking a breath in, say to yourself, silently: *Everyone must die; death cannot be escaped.* Exhale, and stay with those words for several breaths.
3. Repeat: *Everyone must die; death cannot be escaped.* Allow any feelings or sensations to arrive. Notice how it feels to stay with this truth.
4. Again: *Everyone must die; death cannot be escaped.* Not by you, not by anyone else. Breathe in stillness with this first contemplation for a couple minutes.
5. Slowly allow the contemplation, and any accompanying sensations, to drift away. Return to your breathing.

Give yourself several moments to reset. Then it's time for our second contemplation:

1. Take a deep breath and say to yourself: *My life span is continuously getting shorter.* Exhale.
2. Repeat: *My life span is continuously getting shorter.* Day by day, moment by moment, the amount of life we have left is decreasing. Notice how it feels to stay with that truth. There is no right or wrong answer, just allow whatever arises to come. Stay present with it: *My life span is continuously getting shorter.* Each and every day we are closer than ever to our own inevitable end. *My life span is continuously getting shorter.*
3. Stay in stillness with this contemplation for a couple of minutes.
4. Slowly allow the thought, and any accompanying sensations, to drift away. Return to your breathing.

After again taking a few moments, begin the third contemplation. The process should be becoming familiar to you now:

1. Breathing in, say to yourself: *Whether or not I am prepared, my death will come.*
2. Breathing out, let whatever wants to arise do so. *Whether or not I am prepared, my death will come.* If we do not take the time now to prepare, it might someday be too late.
3. Repeat again: *Whether or not I am prepared, my death will come.* Breathe with this contemplation for several moments, allowing any and all sensations to arise.

4. After a while, allow the thought and sensations to fade, and return to your breathing.

Okay, you get how this works. So from here on, I will spare you the detailed instructions and instead give you just the contemplation. Breathe into each one, allow whatever wants to arise to do so, then let it go and rest, before moving on to the next.

- Our fourth contemplation is: *The time of our death is uncertain, I do not know* when *my end will come.*

- Fifth contemplation: *There are many causes of death; I do not know* how *my end will come.*

- Sixth contemplation: *The human body is limited and vulnerable.*

- Seventh contemplation: *At the time of my death, my possessions cannot help me.*

- Eight contemplation: *My loved ones cannot help me escape death.*

- Ninth contemplation: *My own body cannot help me escape death; I will have to leave it behind.*

The first few times you do this practice, end here. Let this be enough.

When you start to feel more experienced with the contemplations, you can dive further in, practicing the nine contemplations first, then continuing as follows. Heads up: things are going to get a *lot* more intense.

1. Thanks to the sixth and ninth contemplations, we have an enhanced awareness that our body is only ours for a finite amount of time. Keeping the lessons of those contemplations fresh in your mind, begin to picture your body.

2. Imagine your body as a lifeless corpse—as if you are outside it, observing it. First see your body as you have seen it in the mirror many times. The only difference is a lack of movement, a lack of breath. What does it feel like to see a body—your body—in stillness, not breathing? Breathe here for several moments, and notice what arises. Then continue.

3. Now, in your mind's eye, watch as the color of your skin starts to fade. What was once glowing and vibrant skin becomes pale and lifeless. Likewise, eyes, nails, and teeth turn gray and dry. The body turns blue, swelling and oozing as the flesh begins to rot. Notice that I'm saying *the* body, not *your* body. It is no longer yours. Breathe here for several moments, then continue.

4. Now, imagine flesh falling away, organs dissipating, until there is nothing left but a skeleton. This pile of bones is all that remains of a body that was once yours. How does it feel to see this once-lively body reduced to a pile of lifeless, white bones? Breathe here for several moments, then continue.

5. At this point envision the bones as they themselves begin to disintegrate, breaking down further and further. All that remains of your former body is dust. How does that feel? Breathe here for several moments.

6. Now the dust blows away. Nothing is left. How does *that* feel? There are no right or wrong answers; we are simply holding space for whatever might arise. Breathe for several moments. Avoid the urge to wrap things up; stay present for a while.

7. After several moments, release all images from your mind's eye. Return to your breathing, then into your body. Wiggle your fingers and toes, allow your head to roll from one shoulder over to the other. Reach your arms overhead, stretch, and then take your time as you bend both knees, roll to one side, and push yourself up into a seated position. Allow your eyes to gently flutter open.

8. Return to your day. It's time to leave this practice behind for now and come back to life, so to speak.

Did you do this practice? If so, I *know* it's brought up some interesting thoughts and reactions in you. I wanna hear all about them, so please find me at facebook.com /miguelgilbertochen and fill me in. Thank you for your practice.

24

Old, Sick, and Dead

Aging, illness, and death are treasures for those who understand them. They're Noble Truths, Noble Treasures. If they were people, I'd bow down to their feet every day.

—AJAAN LEE DHAMMADARO

IMAGINE A WORLD where nobody ever gets sick, grows old, or dies.

A life without pain and without end. This might sound pretty fucking awesome at first. Illness, aging, and dying are to be avoided, right?

Having ill health sucks, that's for sure. No one wants to vomit, get a fever, bleed, or writhe—not for a moment, and certainly not for the rest of their life. But just as we have the ability to change our traditional attitude about death, we can do the same with illness.

It doesn't have to be serious. Take even a common bout of the flu: sure, you feel like shit, you're stuck in bed, and you don't have the energy to get through your to-do list. And yet there's something to be grateful about—if you're open to it. Illness is often life's way of telling us to slow down, take a moment to breathe and be still, and stop taxing our systems unnecessarily. Our bodies give us so much. Through them we can experience the physical world, interact with it and each other. Getting sick is a reminder to appreciate what good health we do have.

As for getting old, things are changing, but it's gonna be a long time before our society stops prizing youth and denigrating what's old. "Old" is a problem to be solved through exercise contraptions, hair dye, "little blue pills," lotions, and vacation packages that will let us stay (or at least maybe feel) young. Billions of dollars spent on—and billions and billions more made by—products that we're told can help us live. It's a lie. Since when does getting older mean we're not living?

Living isn't about age, it's about gratitude and connection. When you reflect on your experiences with the practices in this book, or just times in your life, I'm sure you'll note that there were moments where you felt completely *alive*—and that the feeling wasn't in any way connected to your age. In my own life the sense of connection I derive from my meditation practice is the very same connection I feel when playing a show with my band or looking into my new daughter's eyes. Doesn't matter if I'm a mid-thirties dad or an angst-filled teenager; the connection was, and therefore is, available. If I choose to connect to it, I feel more alive. When I add gratitude to that connection, I feel *very grate-*

fully alive. Nothing to do with age. I felt all this when I was younger, I feel it now, and I know I will if I get older.

Part of the way we make such a big deal about youth is the basic idea that, if you're young, you're further away from death. Well, that's sort of true: right now, you are closer to your own inevitable end than ever before. You could die tomorrow, or you could die fifty years from now—but that's irrelevant to youth, isn't it?

And hey, getting older means more time to accumulate wisdom, more experiences to draw on, more resources with which to connect to life. I'll take that if I'm lucky enough to get it. Which brings us, of course, to death. Wouldn't life, um, be better without it?

Well, it would be longer. But after a few extra decades we'd all just be wrinkly, immobile sacks of dust and farts. "Oh great, here comes my great, great, great, great, great, great-uncle Miguel. He smells." And can you imagine the boredom? Death frees us from a boring, eternal existence of dust-dom. But that's all a silly fantasy anyway. Reality is, our time is finite. It's our most precious resource. You can't make more of it, and you never know when yours will run out. Death gives meaning to whatever amount of time we do have.

If at the end of the day you've "accomplished" a thousand things and connected to zero of them, have you used your previous resources wisely?

Living with a maximum sense of connection means we can die with a minimum sense of regret.

The practices in *The Death of You* have a spiritual or meditative feel, granted. But the sense of connection they foster can be found in countless ways. Eating a *taco de papa* mindfully, enjoying every last bite. Immersing yourself completely in a record or movie. Hiking up a mountain. A family reunion. Painting. Writing. Singing. Telling your S.O. you love them, or really listening to a friend who needs to talk. Or just sitting in silence.

Living fully means connecting to *whatever* the moment may bring—even if it isn't easy or pleasant. We might need to connect to the death of a loved one or our own terminal illness. But if we're open to doing it, it's doable. And that means we don't have to be tortured as we see our last day coming. We've lived as full a life as we reasonably could. Whatever happens next can never erase that.

25

The End

Life is pleasant. Death is peaceful. It's the transition that's troublesome.
                                                    —ISAAC ASIMOV

IT'S ALL OVER. The end of the road. (Or at least the end of the book.)

It'd be nice, I'm sure we agree, if we could wrap up everything we've talked about in a neat little package. But we both know that's not gonna happen. Death won't ever fit into a neat little package. It's a messy, complicated, sometimes awful, sometimes strangely beautiful thing.

I hope this book, and your time with it, has been a reflection of that. We've (hopefully) had some laughs. Maybe we've cried, had moments of discomfort, had some glimpses of peace. Opening up to death give us immediate access to a wide range of emotions. Death is cool like that.

But then, it takes our loved ones from us, breaks our hearts, and causes us unimaginable pain. *Supremely uncool.* When a loved one dies, we can get desperate for answers—answers we probably won't get. Pretty lame of Mister Death, for sure. But even still, death remains one of our greatest potential teachers—our own personal John Keating (that's Robin Williams in *Dead Poets Society*), urging us to *seize the day!* It pushes us to see something great inside of ourselves.

That something great is our tremendous capacity to feel: fear, grief, love, peace.

When we first encounter death, we might be overwhelmed by the sense that nothing will ever be okay again, that life cannot go on. Then something remarkable happens: life does go on. And things do, in a way, become okay again. Death teaches us that we can live full, joyful lives despite, or even because of, its ever-looming presence.

Living a full, joyful life *because of* death might seem like a stretch at first, but I hope I've helped you open up to new possibilities. Like the possibility that we could die any day—and how living with gratitude, all we can, can minimize our fears and maximize what time we have. Death is impermanence embodied, and when we see that clearly, we see how invaluable the present moment really is. We start to appreciate it and avoid mindlessly rushing from one thing to the next. Armed with the knowledge that there won't always be a "next thing" to rush to, we can stop rushing. Death, like life, wants us to be in this moment. Yes, *this* one. Right now. And if there's a next one, that one too.

• • • • •

Death also shows us that despite our endless differences, we are, in a way, all the same. Once we open to it, we begin to know, for real, that:

a) we aren't really alone—even if it really, really feels like it sometimes, and

b) that our supposed differences don't run as deep as we think they might. We all will die, and we'll all feel pain when someone we love dies.

It doesn't matter if someone has a completely different worldview than you, or even if they're a complete asshole. They will encounter death, and their human heart will feel pain because of it. In this way, death reminds us to be more compassionate. To *everyone*. It's perhaps the greatest lesson our teacher has for us.

It doesn't really matter *what kills us*. What matters is *how we die*. And that is inextricably linked with how we've lived. Whether it's an accident or a disease that kills us, whether we can see our death coming for months or it happens in an instant, we *can* die well—if we've lived well. A life of minimal regrets can mean some meaningful modicum of peace in our final moments.

In the meantime, we have to walk a line, asking ourselves, *Are we connecting to death? Are we doing so in a way that our knowledge of it can enhance our lives? Or are we obsessing, trying in vain to understand what will always remain the Great Unknown?* We each have to find our own balance. Part of that means accepting the parts of death that we can't understand. (And would we really want to understand it totally anyway? Isn't there something at least a *little* bit beautiful about the unknown?) Maybe death is something more amazing than we could ever imagine. Or maybe death is completely awful. Maybe death is nothingness, or everything-ness, or something in between. Death's ultimate unknowability is our invitation to focus on the only things that we can even get close to *really* knowing: here and now.

Remember that line from *The Shawshank Redemption*? "Get busy living," it goes, "or get busy dying." It reminds me of a taco commercial (one last taco reference!) where a family is fighting over whether to have hard- or soft-shell tacos for dinner. The youngest daughter saves the day by asking, like some kind of outside-the-box genius, "Why not both?" Result: best family taco night *ever*. So let's follow her brilliant lead and apply it to the get-busy-living-or-dying scenario. I mean, why *not* both?

Life and death are inseparable anyway. So let's get busy.

Oh, and one last tip: watch out for falling elephants. Those things are everywhere.

Thank You

Thanks for reading *The Death of You*. I hope we've shared something that will be of benefit to you and that maybe you can extend to someone you know, to in turn be of benefit to them. And I hope you'll post or message me via facebook .com/miguelgilbertochen with any experiences that came out of your time with the book; it could very well be of benefit to me or someone I know.

Miguel would also like to thank:

My wife, Émilie, and daughter, Olivia, you're my reason for living; my father, Benito; my brothers in Teenage Bottlerocket; the crew at Wisdom Publications; Rod for making my writing suck way less. Party to the people.

Rod would like to thank:

Josh Bartok and the Wisdom Crüe; Larry Rosenberg; and, as always, Maura. Thank you, Flea Foster, for living—

and the way you did it. Most of all, thank *you*, Miguel, for letting me ride shotgun in your big black hearse. It's been a joyride.

Some More Good Books on Death and Other Things We Talked about Here

The Divine Comedy: Inferno; Purgatorio; Paradiso, by Dante Alighieri

Dying with Confidence, by Anyen Rinpoche

The Hour of Our Death: The Classic History of Western Attitudes Toward Death Over the Last One Thousand Years, by Phillippe Ariés

How to Be Sick: A Buddhist-Inspired Guide for the Chronically Ill and Their Caregivers, by Toni Bernhard

I Wanna Be Well: How a Punk Found Peace and You Can Too, by Miguel Chen with Rod Meade Sperry

The Tibetan Book of the Dead: The First Complete Translation, edited by Graham Coleman and Thupten Jinpa;

translated by Gyurme Dorje; introductory commentary by the 14th Dalai Lama

The Oxford Book of Death, chosen and edited by D.J. Enright

The Wheel of Death: Writings from Zen Buddhist and Other Sources, edited by Philip Kapleau Roshi

The Sacred Art of Dying: How World Religions Understand Death, by Kenneth Kramer

On Death & Dying: What the Dying Have to Teach Doctors, Nurses, Clergy & Their Own Families, by Elisabeth Kübler-Ross, M.D.

Who Dies? An Investigation of Conscious Living and Conscious Dying, by Stephen and Ondrea Levine

Making Friends with Death: A Buddhist Guide to Encountering Mortality, by Judith L. Lief

How We Die: Reflections on Life's Final Chapter, by Sherwin B. Nuland

Living in the Light of Death: On the Art of Being Truly Alive, by Larry Rosenberg

The Toltec Art of Life and Death, by Don Miguel Ruiz

The Bodhicaryavatara (Oxford World's Classics), by Santideva; edited by Paul Williams; translated by Kate Crosby and Andrew Skilton

Lessons from the Dying, by Rodney Smith

About the Authors

**MIGUEL CHEN** is the bass player for long-running punk rock band Teenage Bottlerocket, on the Fat Wreck Chords label. He is the author of *I Wanna Be Well: How a Punk Found Peace and You Can Too*. He is an entrepreneur, a meditation practitioner, a yoga instructor, and the founder of Yoga for Punks. In addition to appearing in countless Teenage Bottlerocket press pieces, Miguel has been featured by *Lion's Roar*, *PunkNews*, *Full Contact Enlightenment*, *Dying Scene*, *The One You Feed*, *The Pop Punk Dad*, *Modern Vinyl*, *Chasing Destino*, Chris Grosso's *MindPod* podcast, and more. He lives in Texas with his wife, Émilie; daughter, Olivia; and their two dogs, Stuffing and Cape.

ROD MEADE SPERRY is Miguel's coauthor on *I Wanna Be Well*, the editor of *A Beginner's Guide to Meditation*, and editorial director of LionsRoar.com and Lion's Roar Special Editions. He is a board member of Zen Nova Scotia, the Buddhist community he practices with in his home of Halifax.

What to Read Next
from Wisdom Publications

I Wanna Be Well
How a Punk Found Peace and You Can Too
Miguel Chen and Rod Meade Sperry

"What a wonderful book! I can't recommend it enough."
—Chris Grosso, author of *Indie Spiritualist*

Hardcore Zen
Punk Rock, Monster Movies, and the Truth About Reality
Brad Warner

"*Hardcore Zen* is to Buddhism what the Ramones were to rock and roll: A clear-cut, no-bulls**t offering of truth."
—Miguel Chen, Teenage Bottlerocket

Buddhism for Dudes
A Jarhead's Field Guide to Mindfulness
Gerry Stribling

"*Buddhism for Dudes* shoots straight and doesn't blink. It's John Wayne meets Zen, complete with all the wisdom and tough-guy charm you'd expect."
—Matthew Bortolin, author of *The Dharma of Star Wars*

Unsubscribe
Opt Out of Delusion, Tune In to Truth
Josh Korda

"This book is a how-to guide for people wanting to learn how to face demons, forge deeper connections, sit comfortably in their skin, and step away from the distractions of social media and mindlessness of consumerism—things we all know will never leave us satisfied. Tune in and unsubscribe."
—Cara Buckley of the *New York Times*

Saltwater Buddha
A Surfer's Quest to Find Zen on the Sea
Jaimal Yogis

"Heartfelt, honest, and deceptively simple. It's great stuff with the words 'cult classic' stamped all over it."
—Alex Wade, author of *Surf Nation*

About Wisdom Publications

Wisdom Publications is the leading publisher of classic and contemporary Buddhist books and practical works on mindfulness. To learn more about us or to explore our other books, please visit our website at wisdompubs.org or contact us at the address below.

Wisdom Publications
199 Elm Street
Somerville, MA 02144 USA

We are a 501(c)(3) organization, and donations in support of our mission are tax deductible.

Wisdom Publications is affiliated with the Foundation for the Preservation of the Mahayana Tradition (FPMT).